Cocktails 2007

FOOD&WINE
BOOKS

FOOD & WINE COCKTAILS 2007

EDITOR **Kate Krader**
DEPUTY EDITOR **Jim Meehan**
SENIOR EDITOR **Colleen McKinney**
COPY EDITOR **Kathy Antrim**
RESEARCHER **Maggie Fox**
EDITORIAL ASSISTANTS **Melissa Denchak,
Heather Fox, Athena Theodoro**

ART DIRECTOR **Patricia Sanchez**
DESIGNER **Nancy Blumberg**
DESIGN ASSOCIATE **Katharine Clark**

SENIOR VICE PRESIDENT/CHIEF
MARKETING OFFICER **Mark V. Stanich**
VICE PRESIDENT, BOOKS AND
PRODUCTS **Marshall Corey**
SENIOR MARKETING MANAGER **Bruce Spanier**
ASSISTANT MARKETING MANAGER **Sarah Ross**
PRODUCTION DIRECTOR
Rosalie Abatemarco Samat
CORPORATE PRODUCTION MANAGER
Stuart Handelman
DIRECTOR OF FULFILLMENT **Phil Black**
BUSINESS MANAGER **Tom Noonan**

PHOTOGRAPHY **Tina Rupp**
FOOD STYLING **Alison Attenborough**
PROP STYLING **Dani Fisher**

ON THE COVER All Dave All Night (left), p. 50;
Little Italy, p. 122

ISBN 1-932624-19-8
ISSN 1554-4354

Published by American Express
Publishing Corporation
1120 Avenue of the Americas, New York, NY 10036

Manufactured in the United States of America

FOOD & WINE MAGAZINE

VICE PRESIDENT/EDITOR IN CHIEF **Dana Cowin**
CREATIVE DIRECTOR **Stephen Scoble**
MANAGING EDITOR **Mary Ellen Ward**
EXECUTIVE EDITOR **Pamela Kaufman**
EXECUTIVE FOOD EDITOR **Tina Ujlaki**
EXECUTIVE WINE EDITOR **Lettie Teague**

FEATURES
FEATURES EDITOR **Michelle Shih**
TRAVEL EDITOR **Salma Abdelnour**
SENIOR EDITORS **Ray Isle, Kate Krader**
ASSISTANT EDITORS **Jen Murphy, Ratha Tep**
ASSISTANT HOME & STYLE EDITOR **Dani Fisher**
EDITORIAL ASSISTANTS **Megan Krigbaum,
Jessica Tzerman**

FOOD
SENIOR EDITOR **Kate Heddings**
SENIOR ASSOCIATE EDITOR **Nick Fauchald**
ASSOCIATE EDITOR **Emily Kaiser**
TEST KITCHEN SUPERVISOR **Marcia Kiesel**
SENIOR TEST KITCHEN ASSOCIATE **Grace Parisi**
TEST KITCHEN ASSOCIATE **Melissa Rubel**
EDITORIAL ASSISTANT **Kristin Donnelly**
KITCHEN ASSISTANT **Natalya Buleyev**

ART
ART DIRECTOR **Patricia Sanchez**
SENIOR DESIGNER **Courtney Waddell**
DESIGNER **Michael Patti**
DESIGNER (BOOKS) **Nancy Blumberg**

PHOTO
DIRECTOR OF PHOTOGRAPHY **Fredrika Stjärne**
DEPUTY PHOTO EDITOR **Lucy Schaeffer**
ASSISTANT PHOTO EDITOR **Lisa S. Kim**
PHOTO ASSISTANT **Molly Ryder**

PRODUCTION
ASSISTANT MANAGING EDITOR **Christine Quinlan**
PRODUCTION MANAGER **Matt Carson**
DESIGN/PRODUCTION ASSISTANT **Carl Hesler**

COPY & RESEARCH
COPY CHIEF **Michele Berkover Petry**
SENIOR COPY EDITOR **Ann Lien**
RESEARCH EDITOR **Stacey Nield**
ASSISTANT RESEARCH EDITORS **Kelly Snowden,
Emery Van Hook**

EDITORIAL BUSINESS ASSISTANT **Kalina Mazur**

Cocktails 2007

FOOD & WINE

AMERICAN EXPRESS PUBLISHING CORPORATION, NEW YORK

Contents

Drink up!

We can't decide what's more fun—hanging out in all the excellent bars and lounges we've found in every corner of America, or re-creating their exceptional cocktails at home with the ingredients now available to amateur mixologists. This year, with help from our deputy editor Jim Meehan (one of the country's top bartenders), we perfected over 150 amazing drinks. You'll find those recipes here, along with guides for the most exciting spirits (like Strega, an herb-infused digestif) and mixers (orange bitters). Whether you're ordering a James Bond Martini or shaking up one at home, we hope you're having as much fun as we did.

DANA COWIN
EDITOR IN CHIEF
FOOD & WINE MAGAZINE

KATE KRADER
EDITOR
FOOD & WINE COCKTAILS 2007

Cocktail Clinic

Bar Tools

BOSTON SHAKER

The bartender's choice, consisting of a pint glass with a metal canister that covers the top to create a seal. Measure ingredients into the glass and shake with the metal half pointing away from you. Strain the drink from the canister.

COBBLER SHAKER

The most commonly used shaker, with a metal or glass vessel for mixing drinks with ice, a built-in strainer and a fitted top. Individual shakers accommodate less ice, so they don't chill drinks as well as larger shakers do.

CITRUS JUICER

A shallow dish with a reaming cone, a spout and often a strainer that's used to separate juice from pulp. Juices are best the day they're squeezed, but orange and grapefruit juices can hold for up to two days in the refrigerator.

MUDDLER

A sturdy baseball bat–shaped tool that's used to crush herbs, sugar cubes and fresh fruit. Look for a muddler long enough to reach the bottom of your cocktail shaker; in a pinch, you can use a long-handled wooden spoon.

JIGGER

A two-sided stainless steel measuring instrument. It's indispensable for quick, precise mixing. Look for one with ½- and 1-ounce cups. A shot glass with measurements works well, too.

BAR SPOON

A long-handled metal spoon used to mix and chill cocktails. Stirring doesn't create cloudy air bubbles, so it's preferable for spirits-only drinks, like martinis, which look best crystal clear. It's also useful for measuring small amounts of liquid.

CHANNEL KNIFE

A small spoon-shaped knife with a metal tooth used for peeling long, thin fancy spiral twists from citrus fruit for garnish. A sharp paring knife or vegetable peeler works best for the wider citrus twists that are flamed (p. 121).

WAITER'S CORKSCREW

A pocketknife-like tool with a bottle opener and a small blade used for cutting foil from wine caps. Bartenders prefer this model to the bulkier winged and mechanical corkscrews available.

HAWTHORNE STRAINER

The best all-purpose strainer. This round metal device has a semicircular spring that ensures a snug, spill-proof fit on top of a shaker. Look for a tightly coiled spring, which will keep muddled fruit and herbs out of your drink.

JULEP STRAINER

The preferred device for straining cocktails from a pint glass. Fine holes keep ice out of the finished cocktail, and the shape fits securely inside a mixing glass. In a pinch, though, a Hawthorne strainer will do the trick.

Glassware Arsenal

MARTINI
A long-stemmed glass with a cone-shaped bowl. For cocktails that are served straight up (chilled with ice, then strained).

HIGHBALL
A tall, narrow glass. Helps preserve the fizz in drinks that are served on ice and topped with soda or tonic water.

ROCKS
A short, sturdy, wide-mouthed glass. For spirits served neat and cocktails poured over ice.

RED WINE
A balloon-shaped glass. For fruity cocktails as well as punches; stemless versions are fine stand-ins for snifters.

WHITE WINE
A tall, narrow glass. For wine-based cocktails; a fine substitute for a highball glass.

SNIFTER
A wide-bowled glass designed to rest in your palm. For warm drinks, cocktails served on ice and spirits served neat.

FLUTE
A tall, slender glass whose shape helps keep Champagne and sparkling-wine cocktails effervescent.

PILSNER
A thin, flared glass useful for beer as well as cocktails too large for a highball; can also accommodate multiple garnishes.

COUPE
A shallow, wide-mouthed glass. Primarily used for small (a.k.a. short), potent cocktails.

CORDIAL
A petite, tulip-shaped glass. For powerful drinks served in very small portions, dessert wines and liqueurs served neat.

COLLINS
A taller and narrower glass than a highball. Commonly used for drinks served on ice and topped with a large amount of soda.

PINT
A tall, flared glass with a wide mouth. For stirring or shaking drinks and serving oversize drinks.

Spirits Lexicon

This glossary features many of the spirits in this book. They can be found at most liquor stores and from online retailers like samswine.com, hitimewine.net and astorwines.com.

Amaro A bittersweet Italian herbal liqueur often served as a digestif.

American straight rye whiskey A primarily rye-based distilled spirit that is aged in new charred oak barrels for at least two years.

Aperol A bitter orange Italian aperitif flavored with rhubarb and gentian.

Applejack An American apple brandy often blended with neutral spirits.

Apricot brandy A sweet brandy-based amber liqueur flavored with apricots.

Belle de Brillet A liqueur made by infusing Cognac with macerated Alsatian pears.

Bénédictine A golden herbal liqueur based on a recipe that was developed by French monks in 1510.

Bianco vermouth An aromatic, sweet Italian white vermouth traditionally served on the rocks as an aperitif.

Cachaça A potent Brazilian spirit distilled from fresh sugarcane juice; some of the best are made in copper pot stills and aged in wooden casks.

Campari A bright-red bitter Italian aperitif made from herbs and fruit.

Carpano Antica Formula A rich and complex, crimson-colored sweet Italian vermouth.

Chartreuse A spicy French liqueur made from 130 different herbs; the green version is more potent than the honey-sweetened yellow version.

Cherry Heering A brandy-based Danish cherry liqueur.

Cherry Kijafa A sweet Danish cherry wine that's fortified with brandy.

Creole Shrubb A potent liqueur made by infusing a blend of Martinique rums with bitter orange peel and pulp and Caribbean spices.

Cynar A pleasantly bitter Italian liqueur made from 13 herbs and plants, including artichokes.

Dubonnet red A bittersweet red wine–based aperitif containing spices and quinine that dates back to 1846.

Fernet Branca A bitter Italian digestif made from 27 herbs.

Kümmel A northern European grain-based liqueur flavored with caraway, cumin and fennel.

Licor 43 An orange-and-vanilla-flavored Spanish liqueur made from a combination of 43 herbs and spices.

Lillet Blanc A slightly sweet wine-based French aperitif flavored with orange peel and quinine that was originally marketed as a tonic.

Maraschino liqueur A clear Italian liqueur, the best of which is made from bittersweet marasca cherries, aged in ash barrels for two years, then diluted and sweetened with sugar.

Parfait Amour A purple French liqueur flavored with orange, violets and vanilla.

Pimm's No. 1 A gin-based English aperitif often served with citrus-flavored soda or ginger beer.

Pisco A clear spirit distilled from grapes in the wine-producing regions of Peru and Chile.

Punt e Mes A spicy, orange-accented sweet vermouth fortified with bitters. Its name translates as "point and a half" and refers to the 19th-century Italian tradition of adding dashes (points) of bitters to vermouth.

Rhum agricole An aromatic rum produced in the French West Indies from sugarcane juice. If it's aged from one to six months, it is bottled as rhum blanc; if it's aged for a minimum of three years in oak barrels, it can be sold as *rhum vieux.*

Sherry A fortified wine from Spain's Jerez region. Varieties include dry, fresh styles like fino and Manzanilla; nuttier, richer amontillados and *palo cortados;* and viscous sweet versions such as cream sherry and Pedro Ximénez.

Shochu An unaged or lightly aged, clear East Asian spirit distilled most commonly from rice, barley, buckwheat and/or a variety of sweet potato.

Strega A Sicilian liqueur infused with more than 70 herbs and spices including saffron, which gives it a golden-yellow color.

Tuaca A brandy-based Italian liqueur flavored with vanilla and citrus.

Velvet Falernum A low-alcohol, cane sugar–based liqueur from Barbados flavored with cloves, almond and lime.

Party Playlists

Here are three excellent sound tracks for three different gatherings, with cocktails to match (foodandwine.com/playlists). —*Charlotte Druckman*

Dinner Party for 8

music selections by
Audiostiles's Jeremy Abrams

DRINK

ICED TEA ITALIANO, P. 22

CLOVER CLUB, P. 86

MAN OF LEISURE, P. 119

LISTEN

Charlie Hunter Quartet
More Than This

Jamie Cullum
Wind Cries Mary

Bossacucanova, *Previsão*

Madeleine Peyroux
Don't Wait Too Long

Katie Melua
Just Like Heaven

Feist, *Inside And Out*

Sergio Mendes, *Let Me*
(Remix from *Timeless*)

Paul Anka, *True*

Si Sé, *Mariposa en Havana*

Bent & Billie Holiday, *Speak
Low* (*Bent* Remix)

Cocktail Party for 25

music selections by
restaurateur Stephen Starr

DRINK

RUSH STREET HIGHBALL, P. 84

INDIAN SUMMER, P. 115

APPLE BOMB, P. 132

LISTEN

The Knickerbockers, *Lies*

Wolfmother, *Woman*

Paul Revere & The Raiders
Kicks

Bob Dylan, *Forever Young*

The Killers, *Mr. Brightside*

The Hollies, *Bus Stop*

Joni Mitchell, *River*

T. Rex, *Jeepster*

Neil Young, *Southern Man*

The Ramones, *I Wanna
Be Sedated*

Birthday Bash for 75

music selections by B.R. Guest
music director Todd Mallis

DRINK

ALL DAVE ALL NIGHT, P. 50

BUMBLEBEE, P. 65

AZTECA, P. 98

LISTEN

Dusty Springfield
Wishin' and Hopin'

Les Nubians, *Makeda*

Marcos Valle
Crickets Sing for Anamaria

Andrew Bird, *Skin Is, My*

Gnarls Barkley, *Smiley Faces*

Yo La Tengo
The Race Is On Again

Grand National
Peanut Dreams

The Ditty Bops, *Gentle Sheep*

Phoenix, *If I Ever Feel Better*

Jem, *They*

Cocktail Basics

SIMPLE SYRUP

This bar staple is one of the most universal mixers, essential to many well-balanced cocktails. Stash a jar in your refrigerator; it keeps for up to 1 month.

SIMPLE SYRUP RECIPE

Combine 1 cup of water and 1 cup of sugar in a small saucepan and bring to a boil over moderately high heat, stirring to dissolve the sugar, about 3 minutes. Remove from the heat and let cool. Refrigerate in a tightly covered glass jar until ready to use. Makes about 12 ounces.

CONVERSION CHART

	OUNCES		TABLESPOONS/CUPS
¼	ounce	=	½ tablespoon
½	ounce	=	1 tablespoon
¾	ounce	=	1½ tablespoons
1	ounce	=	2 tablespoons
2	ounces	=	¼ cup
3	ounces	=	¼ cup + 2 tablespoons
4	ounces	=	½ cup
6	ounces	=	¾ cup
8	ounces	=	1 cup
16	ounces	=	2 cups
24	ounces	=	3 cups
32	ounces	=	1 quart

ICED TEA ITALIANO, P. 22
The Tasting Room, New York City

Aperitifs

Pimm's Cooler

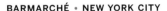

BARMARCHÉ · NEW YORK CITY
Pimm's Cups are traditionally made with lemonade, lemon soda, ginger ale or ginger beer and are garnished lavishly with cucumber, mint leaves and fruit. Former bar manager Ben Scorah's version incorporates Creole Shrubb, an orange liqueur made in Martinique.

2 mint sprigs

2 lemon slices

2 orange slices

1 cucumber wheel, 1 cucumber spear and 1 cucumber ribbon (optional)

1 strawberry, halved

¾ ounce fresh lemon juice

Ice

2 ounces Pimm's No. 1 (English gin-based aperitif)

½ ounce Creole Shrubb or Grand Marnier

3 ounces chilled ginger beer

In a cocktail shaker, muddle the leaves of 1 mint sprig with 1 lemon slice, 1 orange slice, the cucumber wheel, half of the strawberry and the lemon juice. Add ice and the Pimm's and Creole Shrubb. Shake well and strain into an ice-filled pilsner glass. Stir in the ginger beer and garnish with the remaining mint sprig, lemon slice, orange slice, cucumber spear, cucumber ribbon and strawberry half.

PIMM'S COOLER
Barmarché, New York City

Aperitifs

Iced Tea Italiano

THE TASTING ROOM • NEW YORK CITY

Last year, the Tasting Room moved into a larger space with a bar featuring seasonal cocktails and house-made sodas and tonics. This drink is bar manager Richard Ervin's version of the classic Italian summertime cooler.

Ice
2 ounces *amaro* (bittersweet Italian liqueur), such as Meletti
½ ounce fresh lemon juice
2 ounces chilled Prosecco
1 lemon wheel

Fill a rocks glass with ice. Add the *amaro* and lemon juice; stir in the Prosecco. Garnish with the wheel.

The Duke of Bedford

THE LITTLE OWL • NEW YORK CITY

Co-owner Gabriel Stulman used to give a monthly dinner party at his Manhattan apartment, which he called the Blue Blood Café. The Duke of Bedford is a nod to the royal theme.

5 to 6 mint leaves, plus 1 mint sprig
½ ounce Simple Syrup (p. 17)
Ice cubes and crushed ice
3 ounces manzanilla sherry
3 dashes of Angostura bitters
1 ounce chilled *aranciata* (Italian orange soda) or Orangina
1 cucumber wheel

In a pint glass, muddle the mint leaves with the Simple Syrup. Add ice cubes and the sherry, bitters and *aranciata*. Stir well and strain into a highball glass filled with crushed ice. Garnish with the mint sprig and cucumber wheel.

Theresa #4

EASTERN STANDARD · BOSTON
This cocktail is bar manager Jackson Cannon's fourth variation on a drink from Gary Regan's 2003 *The Joy of Mixology.*

8 mint leaves, plus 1 mint sprig
1 ounce crème de cassis
    (black currant liqueur)
Ice
¾ ounce gin
¾ ounce Campari
¾ ounce fresh lime juice
1 ounce chilled club soda

In a cocktail shaker, muddle the mint leaves and crème de cassis. Add ice and the gin, Campari and lime juice. Shake well; strain into an ice-filled highball glass. Stir in the club soda; garnish with the mint sprig.

Pompier

BACCHANALIA · ATLANTA
Pompier is a twist on a cocktail found in Charles H. Baker, Jr.'s 1937 classic, *The Gentleman's Companion.* It substitutes Lillet Blanc for the dry vermouth and gin for the club soda.

Ice
1½ ounces Lillet Blanc
1½ ounces crème de cassis
    (black currant liqueur)
1 ounce gin
1 lemon twist

Fill a pint glass with ice. Add the Lillet, crème de cassis and gin. Stir well and strain into a chilled coupe. Garnish with the lemon twist.

The Parasol

**CATHERINE LOMBARDI •
NEW BRUNSWICK, NJ**
Owners Mark Pascal and
Francis Schott, or "the
Restaurant Guys" as they're
known on their daily radio
show, named their restaurant
after Mark's grandmother
Catherine Lombardi.

½ ounce fresh lemon juice
½ ounce fresh lime juice
¾ ounce Simple Syrup (p. 17)
1 ounce pisco (South American
   grape-based spirit)
2 ounces Aperol or Campari
1 large egg white
Ice
4 drops of Angostura bitters

In a cocktail shaker, combine all
of the ingredients except the ice
and bitters. Shake vigorously for
30 seconds. Add ice, then shake
again. Strain into a chilled martini
glass. Drop 4 dots of bitters onto
the surface of the drink in the
pattern of a square and swirl
gently with a straw or toothpick to
make a design in the foamy head.

THE PARASOL
Catherine Lombardi,
New Brunswick, NJ

Aperitifs

La Sucette

CAFÉ CASTAGNA • PORTLAND, OR
Bar manager Suzanne Allard named La Sucette ("the lollipop") after the French strawberry candy she enjoyed as a child. The recipe calls for Lillet Blanc, a classic aperitif spirit known to stimulate the production of the digestive enzymes that make you feel hungry.

2 strawberries, quartered, plus 1 thin strawberry slice
¼ ounce Simple Syrup (p. 17)
Ice
2½ ounces Lillet Blanc
½ ounce fresh lemon juice

In a pint glass, muddle the quartered strawberries with the Simple Syrup. Add ice and the Lillet and lemon juice; shake well. Strain into a chilled coupe and garnish with the strawberry slice.

Carpano Cocktail

DEL POSTO • NEW YORK CITY
The House of Carpano in Turin, Italy, created one of the first commercially produced sweet vermouths. Mixologist David Slape makes this citrusy drink with Carpano Antica Formula, a newly released vermouth based on Carpano's vintage recipe.

1 cup ice
1½ ounces Carpano Antica Formula or other sweet vermouth
½ ounce Campari
¾ ounce each of fresh lemon juice, lime juice and orange juice
½ ounce Simple Syrup (p. 17)
1 orange twist

Put all of the ingredients except the orange twist in a cocktail shaker. Shake well and pour into a rocks glass. Garnish with the orange twist.

Southern Sweet Breeze

COMMANDER'S PALACE • LAS VEGAS
Mark Silva, former sommelier at the Vegas outpost of New Orleans's legendary Commander's Palace, gathered together three iconic Southern flavors—iced tea, Southern Comfort and peaches— to create this aperitif.

Ice
2 ounces chilled brewed black tea
1½ ounces Southern Comfort
¾ ounce Lillet Blanc
½ ounce fresh lime juice
1 peach slice

Fill a pint glass with ice. Add all of the remaining ingredients except the peach slice; stir well. Strain into an ice-filled pilsner glass. Garnish with the peach slice.

Rooibos Tea Cocktail

P*ONG • NEW YORK CITY
Mixologist Yvan Lemoine, who worked as a pastry chef for years before he stepped behind the bar, creates inspired cocktails like this one—an earthy-fruity combination of South African rooibos tea, the distilled Japanese spirit *shochu* and blackberries.

6 blackberries
½ ounce *shochu*
1 ounce bianco vermouth (sweet white vermouth)
1½ ounces chilled brewed red rooibos tea
Ice
1 lemon twist

In a cocktail shaker, muddle 5 berries with the *shochu,* vermouth and tea. Add ice and stir. Pour through a fine strainer into a chilled coupe. Garnish with the remaining berry and the twist.

MARASCA FIZZ, P. 34
Country, New York City

Wine Cocktails

Wine Cocktails

Bicyclette

OSTERIA PAPAVERO • MADISON, WI
Owner Brian Haltinner adapted this recipe from one at Avenue Restaurant in New York City.

Ice
2 ounces Campari
1½ ounces dry white wine
1 ounce chilled club soda
1 lemon wheel

Fill a pint glass with ice. Add all of the remaining ingredients except the lemon wheel and stir well. Strain into an ice-filled white wine glass and garnish with the lemon wheel.

Bellagio Mist

BELLAGIO POOL BAR • LAS VEGAS
Traditionally a mist refers to an unmixed spirit poured into a glass filled with crushed ice. Mixologist Drew Levinson's mist calls for stirring the ingredients and then straining them over the ice.

Ice cubes and crushed ice
2 ounces dry Riesling
½ ounce amaretto
1½ ounces fresh lemon juice
¾ ounce chilled club soda
½ ounce almond syrup
1 starfruit slice

Fill a pint glass with ice cubes. Add all of the remaining ingredients except the crushed ice and starfruit. Stir well. Strain into a white wine glass filled with crushed ice. Garnish with the starfruit.

Biarritz Cocktail

URBANA • WASHINGTON, DC
Mixologist Jacques Bezuidenhout created this cocktail to complement the Mediterranean cooking at this restaurant next to the Hotel Palomar.

Ice

1¾ ounces gin, preferably Tanqueray No. Ten
1½ ounces Viognier or other aromatic white wine
½ ounce chilled apple juice
¾ ounce fresh lime juice
1 ounce Simple Syrup (p. 17)
1 lemon twist

Fill a cocktail shaker with ice. Add all of the remaining ingredients except the twist. Shake well and strain into an ice-filled highball glass. Garnish with the twist.

Mr. Clean

ROOM 4 DESSERT • NEW YORK CITY
Chef and owner Will Goldfarb named this Champagne cocktail for the piney fresh scent it gets from the mix of lemon and herbal liqueur.

Ice

1 ounce rye
½ ounce green Chartreuse
¾ ounce fresh lemon juice
2 ounces chilled Blanc de Noirs Champagne

Fill a cocktail shaker with ice. Add the rye, Chartreuse and lemon juice; shake well. Strain into a chilled coupe. Stir in the Champagne.

Americana

JP WINE BAR • KANSAS CITY, MO
Almost all of the cocktails at JP incorporate wine; the garnishes are made by chef Darren Bartley, who brandies peaches for this drink.

3 dashes of Peychaud's bitters
1 sugar cube
1 ounce bourbon
4 ounces chilled Champagne
1 tablespoon chopped or sliced
   canned peaches

Sprinkle the bitters over the sugar cube. Pour the bourbon into a chilled flute and top with the Champagne. Add the sugar cube and peaches.

Herbsaint Champagne Cocktail

HERBSAINT • NEW ORLEANS
This Warehouse District restaurant takes its name from the anise-flavored liqueur used in this sparkling cocktail, Herbsaint, which has been made in New Orleans since 1934.

Ice
½ ounce crème de mûre
   (blackberry liqueur)
¼ ounce anise liqueur,
   preferably Herbsaint
4 ounces chilled Champagne
1 lemon twist

Fill a pint glass with ice. Add the crème de mûre and anise liqueur and stir well. Strain into a chilled flute and top with the Champagne. Garnish with the lemon twist.

AMERICANA
JP Wine Bar, Kansas City, MO

Marasca Fizz

COUNTRY • NEW YORK CITY
Country offers 50 sparkling wines by the bottle and up to 6 by the glass. For this Champagne cocktail, the restaurant soaks pitted sweet cherries in an anise-infused syrup.

3　maraschino cherries, plus
　　¾ ounce syrup from the jar
Superfine sugar
3　dashes of Angostura bitters
2　brown sugar cubes
½　ounce Cherry Heering
　　or cherry liqueur
4　ounces chilled Champagne

Moisten the outer rim of a flute with ½ ounce maraschino cherry syrup and coat with superfine sugar. Sprinkle the bitters over the sugar cubes. Add the Cherry Heering, maraschino cherries and the remaining ¼ ounce maraschino cherry syrup to the flute. Top with the Champagne and add the sugar cubes.

Mid-Autumn Highball

TRINA RESTAURANT & LOUNGE • FORT LAUDERDALE

"I love the combination of mint and apple," says cocktail consultant Nick Mautone. "So I experimented and came up with several cocktails. This version is my personal favorite."

6 mint leaves, plus 1 mint sprig
¾ ounce Simple Syrup (p. 17)
Ice
½ ounce green Chartreuse
1½ ounces citrus rum
3 ounces alcoholic sparkling apple cider

In a cocktail shaker, muddle the mint leaves with the Simple Syrup. Add ice and the Chartreuse and rum; shake well. Stir in the cider. Strain into an ice-filled highball glass. Garnish with the sprig.

Bellini

KATSUYA • LOS ANGELES

The pink-hued Bellini was created in the late 1940s by Giuseppe Cipriani at Harry's Bar in Venice. It was named after 15th-century Italian artist Giovanni Bellini, whose signature works had a pink glow.

3 thyme sprigs
¼ ounce Simple Syrup (p. 17)
Ice
1 ounce peach puree or nectar
Dash of peach bitters
4 ounces chilled Prosecco

In a pint glass, muddle 2 thyme sprigs with the Simple Syrup. Add all of the remaining ingredients except the last thyme sprig. Stir well and strain into a chilled flute. Garnish with the remaining thyme sprig.

Sparkling Mint

FRANNY'S • BROOKLYN, NY
Francine Stephens was a bartender for years at the restaurant Savoy in Manhattan before she opened Franny's, the exceptional Brooklyn trattoria, with her husband, chef Andrew Feinberg.

3 mint leaves
½ ounce Mint Syrup (below)
Ice
½ ounce Cynar (artichoke liqueur)
½ ounce fresh lime juice
3 ounces chilled Prosecco

In a pint glass, muddle the mint leaves with the Mint Syrup. Add ice and the Cynar, lime juice and Prosecco and stir well. Strain into a chilled flute.

MINT SYRUP In a small saucepan, bring 6 ounces Simple Syrup (p. 17) to a boil. Remove from the heat and add 20 mint leaves. Let cool, then refrigerate overnight. Strain the syrup into an airtight container and refrigerate for up to 3 weeks. Makes 6 ounces.

The Shogun ♼

ZOLA • WASHINGTON, DC
"Sake is difficult to work with in cocktails," says mixologist Ralph Rosenberg. "The flavor usually gets covered up." Here, gingery lemonade adds spice without overpowering the lychee-scented sake, which is called Buna no Tsuyu ("Dewdrops").

MAKES 10 DRINKS

- 25 ounces sake (about 750 ml), preferably *junmai*
- 10 ounces Ginger Lemonade (below)
- 5 ounces Cointreau or other triple sec
- 10 canned lychees, drained
- 5 teaspoons chilled strong-brewed hibiscus tea

In a pitcher, combine the sake, Ginger Lemonade and Cointreau. Cover and refrigerate until chilled, at least 2 hours. Put 1 lychee in each of 10 chilled martini glasses. Stir the sake-lemonade mixture and pour into the prepared martini glasses. Pour ½ teaspoon hibiscus tea on top of each drink.

GINGER LEMONADE In a pitcher, stir ¾ cup fresh lemon juice and ¼ cup plus 2 tablespoons water with 3 tablespoons Ginger Syrup (p. 64). Cover and refrigerate for up to 2 days. Makes 10½ ounces.

Pear-adise

GINGER GROVE • COCONUT GROVE, FL
You can order this drink at the restaurant Ginger Grove, located on the second floor of the Mayfair Hotel & Spa, at the lounge on the ground floor or at the rooftop bar, where private cabanas outfitted with plasma TVs are used for massages by day and as cocktail nooks at night.

Ice

1½ ounces Ginger-Infused Vodka (below)

½ ounce pear liqueur

1 ounce sake

1 ounce pear nectar

1 thin pear slice

Fill a cocktail shaker with ice. Add all of the remaining ingredients except the pear slice. Shake well and strain into a chilled martini glass. Garnish with the pear slice.

GINGER-INFUSED VODKA In an airtight container, cover 4 ounces peeled and diced fresh ginger with 1 cup vodka. Refrigerate for 3 days, then strain into another container. Refrigerate for up to 2 weeks. Makes 8 ounces.

Pear Flower

MINT/820 • PORTLAND, OR

Just as chefs work with farmers to sustain local agriculture, mixologists such as Mint/820 owner Lucy Brennan are working with local distilleries—like Oregon's SakéOne, which makes the Moonstone pear sake she uses in this drink—to help support the growth of artisanal spirits produced in the U.S.

Ice

1½   ounces pear sake
1   ounce vodka
½   ounce fresh lemon juice
½   ounce fresh lime juice
1   ounce Jasmine Syrup (below)

Fill a cocktail shaker with ice. Add all of the remaining ingredients. Shake well and strain into a chilled martini glass.

JASMINE SYRUP In a small saucepan, bring 6 ounces Simple Syrup (p. 17) to a boil. Remove from the heat and add 1 jasmine tea bag. Let steep for 5 minutes. Remove the tea bag, let the syrup cool, then refrigerate in an airtight container for up to 3 weeks. Makes 6 ounces.

**VODKA-THYME
LEMONADE (LEFT), P. 56**
Perry St., New York City
SHISO-JITO, P. 53
Morimoto, Philadelphia

Vodka

Vodka

Smashed Cherry Lemonade

COOKSHOP · NEW YORK CITY
Bar manager Lateefah Curtis serves this drink with fresh bing cherries in summer to complement chefs Marc Meyer and Joel Hough's Greenmarket-driven New American menu.

5 bing or brandied cherries
4 lemon wedges
1 ounce Simple Syrup (p. 17)
Ice
2 ounces vodka
½ ounce fresh lemon juice
1 ounce chilled club soda

In a cocktail shaker, muddle 4 cherries, 3 lemon wedges and the Simple Syrup. Add ice and the vodka and lemon juice. Shake well; strain into an ice-filled highball glass. Stir in the soda. Garnish with the last cherry and lemon wedge.

Apple Drink

SONA · LOS ANGELES
Owner David Myers's Apple Drink is a hybrid of two hyper-popular cocktails from the past decade: the fruit-flavored martini and the mojito.

7 mint leaves
1 canned lychee, drained
1½ ounces chilled apple cider
Ice
2 ounces vodka
1 apple slice

In a cocktail shaker, muddle the mint leaves with the lychee and cider. Add ice and the vodka. Shake well; strain into an ice-filled rocks glass. Garnish with the apple slice.

La Vie en Rose

CUSTOM HOUSE · CHICAGO
The inspiration for the unlikely combination of flavors in this cocktail came when a colleague of bar manager Tim Lacey said he tasted hints of rosemary in the framboise.

1½ teaspoons rosemary leaves
½ ounce Simple Syrup (p. 17)
Ice
1½ ounces vodka
1 ounce framboise
1 ounce Lillet Blanc
1 raspberry

In a cocktail shaker, muddle the rosemary with the Simple Syrup. Add ice and the vodka, framboise and Lillet. Stir well and strain into a chilled coupe. Garnish with the raspberry.

Chocolate-Pear Martini

RADIUS · BOSTON
This drink is loosely based on the 20th Century cocktail, created by British bartender C.A. Tuck for the famous 20th Century Limited train, which ran from New York to Chicago from 1902 to 1967 and carried passengers such as Theodore Roosevelt, "Diamond Jim" Brady and J.P. Morgan.

1 pear slice and cocoa powder
Ice
2 ounces vodka
1 ounce Belle de Brillet or pear liqueur
½ ounce fresh lime juice
½ ounce white crème de cacao

Moisten the outer rim of a martini glass with the pear slice and coat lightly with cocoa. Fill a cocktail shaker with ice. Add all of the remaining ingredients. Shake well; strain into the martini glass.

Vodka

Le Midi

SAMBAR · SEATTLE
Co-owner and pastry chef
Sara Naftaly transformed
her studio apartment into
this cocktail lounge and
began serving drinks like
Le Midi, flavored with a variety
of Provençal lavenders.

MAKES 6 DRINKS

¾ pound blueberries
1 cup Simple Syrup (p. 17)
½ ounce fresh lemon juice
½ ounce Grand Marnier
Ice
9 ounces vodka
4½ ounces fresh lime juice
1½ ounces Lavender Syrup (below)
6 fresh lavender sprigs

In a medium saucepan, combine the blueberries with the Simple Syrup and lemon juice. Cook over moderately high heat until the berry skins darken, 1 to 2 minutes. Drain the berries, reserving the syrup. In a pitcher, combine the berries, half the syrup and all of the remaining ingredients except the lavender sprigs. Cover and refrigerate until chilled. Stir and strain into 6 chilled martini glasses. Garnish with the lavender sprigs.

LAVENDER SYRUP In a small saucepan, bring 6 ounces Simple Syrup (p. 17) to a boil. Remove from the heat and add 2 teaspoons dried lavender. Let cool, then refrigerate overnight. Strain the syrup and refrigerate for up to 3 weeks. Makes 6 ounces.

LE MIDI
Sambar, Seattle

Rosemary Martini

JEFFREY'S RESTAURANT & BAR •
AUSTIN, TX

When bar manager Mark Grubb took his position at Jeffrey's, he faced the age-old task of managing the bar's inventory. Part of that inventory included four cases of an obscure and delicious sparkling pear cider that wasn't selling, so he created this drink to move some stock.

Ice
2 ounces vodka
1 ounce Rosemary Syrup (below)
¾ ounce fresh lemon juice
½ ounce chilled sparkling pear or apple cider
1 lemon wheel

Fill a cocktail shaker with ice. Add the vodka, Rosemary Syrup and lemon juice. Shake well, stir in the sparkling pear cider and strain into a chilled martini glass. Float the lemon wheel on the surface of the drink.

ROSEMARY SYRUP In a small saucepan, bring 6 ounces Simple Syrup (p. 17) to a boil. Remove from the heat and add 2 rosemary sprigs. Let cool, then refrigerate overnight. Strain the syrup into an airtight container and refrigerate for up to 3 weeks. Makes 6 ounces.

Cocktail al Souk

AGRARIA · WASHINGTON, DC

Mixologist Derek Brown's goal with this cocktail was to capture the colors, tastes and smells of the wonderful ingredients sold in the souks of Morocco.

Ice

1½ ounces Fig Vodka (below)
 ½ ounce amaretto
  2 drops of rose flower water
  2 dashes of mint bitters
  1 mint leaf

Fill a pint glass with ice. Add all of the remaining ingredients except the mint leaf. Stir well and strain into a chilled coupe. Float the mint leaf on the surface of the drink.

FIG VODKA In an airtight container, cover 6 dried figs with 1 cup vodka. Refrigerate for 4 days. Strain the vodka through a coffee filter and refrigerate in an airtight container for up to 1 week. Makes 8 ounces.

Vodka

El Gato Negro

RESTAURANT MAGNUS ·
MADISON, WI
Port was used in a number
of early-20th-century
cocktails but fell out of favor
until recently, when wine-
oriented mixologists
like Finn Berge began using
it to replace vermouth.

Ice

2 ounces tawny port
1 ounce crème de mûre
  (blackberry liqueur)
2 ounces vodka
1 lemon twist and 1 brandied cherry

Fill a cocktail shaker with ice. Add the
port, crème de mûre and vodka. Stir
well and strain into a chilled coupe.
Garnish with the twist and cherry.

The Charleston Cocktail

HIGH COTTON · **CHARLESTON, SC**
Beverage director Patrick
Emerson created this drink for
a cocktail competition held
by a local vodka company. The
Madeira he uses is the Rare
Wine Co.'s Charleston Sercial,
which was fashioned after
the delicate Madeiras that
Charlestonians drank in the
18th and 19th centuries.

Ice cubes, plus crushed ice

1½ ounces vodka
½ ounce Sercial Madeira, such as Blandy's
2 ounces chilled brewed black tea
1 ounce fresh lemon juice
½ ounce Simple Syrup (p. 17)
½ ounce Mint Syrup (p. 36)
½ ounce water
1 mint sprig

Fill a cocktail shaker with ice cubes. Add
all of the remaining ingredients except
the crushed ice and mint sprig. Shake
well; strain into a pilsner glass filled with
crushed ice. Garnish with the mint sprig.

Players Cup

RANGE • SAN FRANCISCO
The word *cocktail* encompasses all kinds of mixed drinks, including fixes, crustas, cobblers, flips, juleps and punches. Cups were a category of fancy drinks made with wine or spirits and garnished lavishly with fruit.

1 cup ice
2 ounces vodka
1 ounce Grand Marnier
1 ounce fresh lime juice
2 dashes of Angostura bitters
4 raspberries
4 to 5 mint leaves, plus 1 mint sprig
3 thin cucumber wheels
1 ounce chilled ginger ale

In a cocktail shaker, combine all of the ingredients except the mint sprig, 1 cucumber wheel and the ginger ale and shake well. Pour into a pilsner glass, stir in the ginger ale and garnish with the mint sprig and cucumber wheel.

Vodka

All Dave All Night

BARNDIVA • HEALDSBURG, CA
Bartender Dave Nucelli invented this drink one night while working a double shift. "The drink is refreshing and has a long finish," says general manager Lukka Feldman, "just like our Dave."

Ice

3 ounces orange vodka, preferably Hangar One Mandarin Blossom
1 ounce fresh lime juice
½ ounce elderflower syrup
1 orange twist

Fill a cocktail shaker with ice. Add the vodka, lime juice and elderflower syrup. Shake well and strain into a chilled martini glass. Garnish with the twist.

The Fresca

THE RED CAT • NEW YORK CITY
When the Red Cat opened in 1999, owner Jimmy Bradley searched in vain for hard-to-find sodas such as Fresca (his childhood favorite). He was thrilled when his bartender created this cocktail, which approximates Fresca's citrusy flavor.

Ice

3 ounces orange vodka
1 ounce Cointreau or other triple sec
¾ ounce fresh grapefruit juice
½ ounce fresh lime juice
½ ounce chilled 7-UP
1 orange twist

Fill a cocktail shaker with ice. Add all of the remaining ingredients except the 7-UP and twist. Shake well, stir in the 7-UP and strain into a chilled martini glass. Garnish with the twist.

ALL DAVE ALL NIGHT
Barndiva, Healdsburg, CA

Vodka

Smooth Operator

PROVIDENCE • **LOS ANGELES**
This cocktail was named by bartender Vincenzo Marianella's wife, who tried the drink while the song "Smooth Operator" by Sade was playing.

5   seedless red grapes, plus 3 red grapes skewered on a pick
½   ounce Simple Syrup (p. 17)
Ice
2   ounces honey vodka
½   ounce honey liqueur, such as Bärenjäger
1   ounce fresh lemon juice

In a cocktail shaker, muddle the 5 grapes with the Simple Syrup. Add ice and the vodka, honey liqueur and lemon juice. Shake well and strain into a chilled martini glass. Garnish with the skewered grapes.

Sienna Sunset

LICOROUS • **SEATTLE**
This drink is a collaboration between mixologist Michelle Magidow, who infused the vodka with cinnamon, and general manager Tim Johnstone, who had the idea to mix it with Tuaca, a vanilla-spiked liqueur.

Ice
1½   ounces cinnamon vodka
½   ounce Tuaca (vanilla-flavored liqueur)
1   ounce orange juice
½   ounce chilled club soda
1   orange slice

Fill a cocktail shaker with ice. Add the vodka, Tuaca and orange juice. Shake well and strain into an ice-filled highball glass. Stir in the club soda and garnish with the orange slice.

Smith & Thomas

EMERIL'S ATLANTA · ATLANTA
Bartender Regan Smith and bar manager Curt Thomas created this cocktail for a party in honor of local celebrity Tom Houck, who was Martin Luther King, Jr.'s driver.

Ice
2 ounces chilled brewed black tea
1½ ounces raspberry vodka
½ ounce limoncello (lemon-flavored liqueur)
½ ounce cranberry juice
¼ ounce Simple Syrup (p. 17)
3 raspberries, skewered on a pick

Fill a pilsner glass with ice. Add all of the remaining ingredients except the berries; stir well. Garnish with the berries.

Shiso-Jito

MORIMOTO · PHILADELPHIA
Bar manager Emily Leveen replaces the mint in this mojito with shiso, the spiky-leaved Asian herb. "The sushi chefs here clap it between their hands to release the aroma," says Leveen. "I just tear it."

3 shiso or mint leaves, 2 torn into 4 pieces each
2 lime wedges
1 teaspoon chopped candied ginger
Ice
2 ounces citrus vodka
1 ounce chilled ginger ale

In a cocktail shaker, muddle the torn shiso and lime wedges with the candied ginger. Add ice and the vodka. Shake well; strain into an ice-filled rocks glass. Stir in the ginger ale and garnish with the shiso leaf.

Passionflower

CLUB PRIVÉ • LAS VEGAS

This cocktail gets its "passion" from Parfait Amour ("perfect love"), a sweet violet liqueur flavored with violet petals, orange peel and vanilla bean.

Ice
1½ ounces citrus vodka
¾ ounce Campari
½ ounce Parfait Amour (purple-hued violet-flavored liqueur)
¾ ounce fresh lemon juice
1 large egg white
1 edible orchid or 1 lime wheel

Fill a cocktail shaker with ice. Add all of the remaining ingredients except the orchid; shake vigorously. Strain into an ice-filled highball glass. Garnish with the orchid.

Tranquillity

BUDDAKAN • NEW YORK CITY

At this dramatic 16,000-square-foot Asian restaurant, Tranquillity can be ordered in the library, the cocktail lounge, the Louis XIV–inspired dining room or the brasserie, where hundreds of images of Buddha line the walls.

Ice
1½ ounces citrus vodka
2 ounces chilled brewed oolong tea
½ ounce Lemongrass Syrup (p. 93)
½ ounce Citrus Syrup (p. 152)
1 lemon wedge

Fill a cocktail shaker with ice. Add all of the ingredients except the lemon wedge. Shake well and strain into an ice-filled highball glass. Garnish with the lemon wedge.

PASSIONFLOWER
Club Privé, Las Vegas

Vodka

Vodka-Thyme Lemonade

PERRY ST. • NEW YORK CITY

This subtle variation on a Vodka Collins—lemon juice, sugar, vodka and soda—pairs well with the clean, light flavors in star chef Jean-Georges Vongerichten's Asian-inflected cooking.

4 lemon wedges and superfine sugar

Ice

2 ounces Lemon-Thyme Syrup (below)

2 ounces citrus vodka

1 ounce chilled club soda

1 lemon thyme sprig

Moisten the outer rim of a highball glass with 1 lemon wedge and coat lightly with superfine sugar. Add ice to the glass. In a cocktail shaker, muddle the remaining 3 lemon wedges with the Lemon-Thyme Syrup. Add ice and the vodka and shake well. Stir in the club soda. Strain the drink into the prepared highball glass and garnish with the lemon thyme sprig.

LEMON-THYME SYRUP In a small saucepan, bring 6 ounces Simple Syrup (p. 17) to a boil. Remove from the heat and add 7 lemon thyme sprigs. Let cool, then refrigerate overnight. Strain the syrup into an airtight container and refrigerate for up to 3 weeks. Makes 6 ounces.

Star Anise Lemon Drop

SUMMIT · COLORADO SPRINGS
To make the Star Anise Lemon Drop, the bartenders at Summit use Hangar One Buddha's Hand citron vodka, infused with the fragrant oil from the peel and pith of the "fingers" of the unusually shaped seedless and juiceless Buddha's Hand fruit.

1 lemon wedge and cardamom sugar mix (3 tablespoons superfine sugar with 1 tablespoon ground cardamom)

Ice

1½ ounces citrus vodka

1 ounce Star Anise Syrup (below)

¾ ounce fresh lemon juice

¾ ounce Cointreau or other triple sec

1 star anise pod

Moisten the outer rim of a martini glass with the lemon wedge and coat lightly with the cardamom sugar. Fill a cocktail shaker with ice. Add the vodka, Star Anise Syrup, lemon juice and Cointreau. Shake well and strain into the prepared martini glass. Garnish with the star anise pod.

STAR ANISE SYRUP In a small saucepan, bring 6 ounces Simple Syrup (p. 17) to a boil. Remove from the heat and add 3 whole star anise pods. Let cool, then refrigerate overnight. Strain the syrup into an airtight container and refrigerate for up to 3 weeks. Makes 6 ounces.

PHILADELPHIA FISH HOUSE PUNCH, P. 68
Bobby Flay Steak, Atlantic City

Rum

Rum

The Santa Cruz Rum Daisy

LITTLE BRANCH • NEW YORK CITY
Santa Cruz rum is a historic name for the light rums of the Virgin Islands. A daisy is a classic type of drink that usually includes a spirit, lemon juice, soda and a sweetener such as simple syrup, curaçao or grenadine.

Ice

2 ounces light rum
¾ ounce orange curaçao
¾ ounce fresh lemon juice
1 lemon twist

Fill a cocktail shaker with ice. Add the rum, curaçao and lemon juice; shake well. Strain into a chilled martini glass. Squeeze the twist over the drink, rub it around the rim of the glass, then discard it.

Peach Rum Old-Fashioned

NOPA • SAN FRANCISCO
This variation on an old-fashioned is featured on Nopa's seasonal bar menu during June and July, when peaches are at their peak.

1 peach slice
1 orange slice
3 brandied cherries
½ ounce cane syrup, such as Depaz
3 dashes of Angostura bitters
1 cup ice
1½ ounces amber rum

In a pint glass, muddle the peach, orange and cherries with the syrup and bitters. Add the ice and rum and pour back and forth between the pint glass and a rocks glass 3 times. Pour into the rocks glass.

Anjou Pear Mojito

HUGO'S • HOUSTON
Calvados is a French brandy made from apples that can come only from Normandy. "Classic, old-world spirits are not made, they're grown," says mixologist Sean Beck, who uses the familiar mojito to turn people on to this refined spirit.

2 mint sprigs
¾ ounce pear nectar
Ice
1½ ounces amber rum
½ ounce Calvados
¾ ounce fresh lime juice
¾ ounce Simple Syrup (p 17)
1 ounce chilled club soda
1 pear slice

In a cocktail shaker, muddle the leaves from 1 mint sprig with the pear nectar. Add ice and the rum, Calvados, lime juice and Simple Syrup. Shake well and strain into an ice-filled rocks glass. Stir in the club soda. Garnish with the remaining mint sprig and the pear slice.

Rum

Halekulani Melon Daiquiri

LEWERS LOUNGE · HONOLULU
This drink is based on a fancy nonalcoholic drink famed mixologist Dale DeGroff concocted at New York City's Rainbow Room. DeGroff uses orange bitters and amber rum to add spice and depth.

1½ ounces amber rum
¼ cantaloupe—peeled, seeded and cut into cubes, plus 1 cantaloupe wedge
1 ounce Simple Syrup (p. 17)
1 ounce fresh lime juice
Dash of orange bitters
6 ounces crushed ice
1 mint sprig

In a blender, puree all of the ingredients except the cantaloupe wedge and mint sprig. Pour into a snifter and garnish with the cantaloupe wedge and mint sprig.

Cuban Manhattan

LONDON GRILL · PHILADELPHIA
London Grill owner Terry McNally grew up in Puerto Rico and loves drinking rum. Her house specialty is a variation on a Manhattan, which substitutes rum for whiskey.

Ice
2½ ounces amber rum
¾ ounce Cherry Kijafa or sweet vermouth
3 brandied cherries, skewered on a pick

Fill a pint glass with ice. Add the rum and Cherry Kijafa and stir well. Strain into a chilled martini glass; garnish with the brandied cherries.

HALEKULANI MELON DAIQUIRI
Lewers Lounge, Honolulu

Rum

The Trenchtown

MARJORIE • SEATTLE
When owner Donna Moodie was growing up in Jamaica, her father worked for Appleton Estate, which makes the rum she uses in this drink.

Ice
2 ounces amber rum
1 ounce coconut water
1 ounce fresh lime juice
1 ounce Ginger Syrup (below)
1 lime wheel

Fill a cocktail shaker with ice. Add all of the remaining ingredients except the lime wheel and shake well. Strain into a chilled martini glass. Garnish with the lime wheel.

GINGER SYRUP In a small saucepan, bring 6 ounces Simple Syrup (p. 17) to a boil. Remove from the heat and add 1 ounce peeled and diced fresh ginger. Let cool, then refrigerate overnight. Strain the syrup into an airtight container and refrigerate for up to 3 weeks. Makes 6 ounces.

St. Louis #1

BRANDY LIBRARY • NEW YORK CITY
This cocktail is the first of a series of cocktails named after three New Orleans cemeteries (St. Louis #1, #2 and #3) thought to be haunted.

Ice
2 ounces amber rum
1 ounce Creole Shrubb or Grand Marnier
½ ounce Simple Syrup (p. 17)
½ ounce fresh lime juice
Dash of orange bitters
1 orange twist

Fill a cocktail shaker with ice. Add all of the remaining ingredients except the orange twist and shake well. Strain into a chilled martini glass. Garnish with the twist.

Bumblebee

COCOLIQUOT • MADISON, WI
Owner Brian Haltinner named this variation on the Dark & Stormy after the spicy sting of the ginger beer.

Ice
2 ounces amber rum
1 ounce Grand Marnier
¾ ounce fresh lime juice
2 ounces chilled ginger beer
1 lime wheel

Fill a cocktail shaker with ice. Add the rum, Grand Marnier and lime juice and shake well. Strain into an ice-filled collins glass; stir in the ginger beer. Garnish with the wheel.

Canton

ZIG ZAG CAFE • SEATTLE
Zig Zag owners Ben Dougherty and Kacy Fitch and bartender Murray Stenson love obscure and out-of-print bartending books. This drink comes from one of their favorites: *Jones's Complete Barguide,* published in 1977.

Ice
3 ounces amber rum
½ ounce maraschino liqueur (bittersweet cherry liqueur)
½ ounce Cointreau or other triple sec
½ teaspoon grenadine, preferably Homemade Grenadine (below)
1 maraschino cherry and 1 orange twist

Fill a cocktail shaker with ice. Add all of the remaining ingredients except the cherry and orange twist. Stir and strain into a chilled coupe. Garnish with the cherry and orange twist.

HOMEMADE GRENADINE In a large saucepan, combine 32 ounces pomegranate juice, ½ pound superfine sugar and the seeds from half of a pomegranate and simmer until the juice has reduced by half. Let cool, strain into an airtight container and stir in ⅛ teaspoon citric acid powder (see Note). Refrigerate for up to 1 month. Makes about 16 ounces.

NOTE Citric acid, which is found in many kinds of fruit, preserves food and adds acidity. It's available in powdered form at health food stores or at bestturkishfood.com (p. 215).

Creole Napoleon

NATT SPIL · MADISON, WI
Bartender Michael Reynolds created this drink for the playfully misspelled Natt Spil, which literally means "night play," and refers to the bars that Norwegians frequent after a night at a club.

1½ teaspoons minced peeled fresh ginger
1 dash of Peychaud's bitters
Ice
2 ounces Creole Shrubb or Grand Marnier
2 ounces chilled club soda
1 ounce dark rum, preferably Gosling's
1 mint leaf and 1 lime wedge

In a rocks glass, muddle the ginger with the bitters. Add ice and the Creole Shrubb. Stir in the club soda. Pour the rum over a bar spoon on top. Garnish with the mint leaf and lime wheel.

Malta Fizz

WD-50 · NEW YORK CITY
Head bartender Jose "Juice" Miranda based the Malta Fizz on a traditional Latin American drink his mother made for him as a child with egg yolk, sugar, condensed milk and malta, a nonalcoholic carbonated malt beverage available at Latin American markets.

Ice
2 ounces amber rum
2 ounces malta
¾ ounce fresh lime juice
1 ounce Simple Syrup (p. 17)
1 large egg yolk
Pinch of ground cinnamon

Fill a cocktail shaker with ice. Add all of the remaining ingredients except the cinnamon; shake vigorously for 30 seconds. Strain into an ice-filled collins glass. Garnish with the cinnamon.

Rum

Philadelphia Fish House Punch

BOBBY FLAY STEAK · ATLANTIC CITY

Cocktail historians Paul Harrington and Laura Moorhead trace this cocktail back to 1732, when Philadelphia's Schuylkill Fishing Club began every meeting with a bowl of this potent punch.

Ice
¾ ounce dark rum
¾ ounce Cognac
¾ ounce peach brandy
½ ounce Simple Syrup (p. 17)
¼ ounce fresh lime juice
½ ounce fresh lemon juice
1 lime slice and 1 maraschino cherry

Fill a cocktail shaker with ice. Add all of the remaining ingredients except the lime slice and cherry. Shake well; strain into an ice-filled rocks glass. Garnish with the lime slice and cherry.

Sandía

THE MODERN · NEW YORK CITY

The bar team at The Modern invented the Sandía ("watermelon" in Spanish) with summer in mind. Most of the restaurant's cocktails pair well with food; this one complements fish, especially salmon.

2 ounces melon rum
1 dill sprig
2 lemon wedges, halved crosswise
Three 1-inch cantaloupe cubes
1 cup ice
1 ounce chilled tonic water

In a cocktail shaker, muddle the rum with the dill sprig, lemon wedges and cantaloupe cubes. Add the ice, shake well and pour into a rocks glass. Stir in the tonic water.

SANDÍA
The Modern, New York City

Earl Grey Boxcar

BONG SU • SAN FRANCISCO
The cocktails at Bong Su incorporate Southeast Asian ingredients like lemongrass, kaffir limes and Earl Grey tea.

Ice
1¼ ounces Earl Grey Rum (below)
½ ounce Punt e Mes
   (bittersweet vermouth)
½ ounce pineapple juice
¼ ounce apricot brandy
¼ ounce Simple Syrup (p. 17)
1 dash of Angostura bitters
½ ounce fresh lemon juice
½ ounce fresh lime juice
1 lemon wheel

Fill a cocktail shaker with ice. Add all of the remaining ingredients except the lemon wheel and shake well. Strain into a chilled martini glass and float the lemon wheel on the surface of the drink.

EARL GREY RUM Add 2 Earl Grey tea bags to 8 ounces citrus rum and let stand for 45 minutes. Discard the tea bags and pour into an airtight container. Refrigerate for up to 1 month. Makes 8 ounces.

Cable Car

SIBLING RIVALRY • BOSTON

The Cable Car was created by mixologist Tony Abou-Ganim in 1996 as a signature drink for Harry Denton's Starlight Room, a famous cocktail lounge on the top floor of the Sir Francis Drake Hotel in San Francisco.

1 lemon wedge and superfine sugar
Ice
2 ounces spiced rum
¾ ounce orange curaçao
1 ounce fresh lemon juice
1 orange twist

Moisten the outer rim of a martini glass with the lemon wedge and coat with sugar. Fill a cocktail shaker with ice. Add the rum, curaçao and lemon juice; shake well. Strain into the martini glass; garnish with the twist.

Apple Smack

HYDE LOUNGE • LOS ANGELES

The bartenders at Hyde Lounge use chai-flavored apple preserves in this spiced drink, making it a great cocktail for fall and winter.

Ice
2 ounces rhum agricole
   (aromatic West Indian rum)
½ ounce apple butter
1 ounce fresh lime juice
½ ounce Simple Syrup (p. 17)
1 dried apple ring and grated nutmeg

Fill a cocktail shaker with ice. Add all of the remaining ingredients except the apple ring and nutmeg; shake well. Strain into a chilled martini glass. Garnish with the apple and nutmeg.

Rum

Ti Punch

CLARK STREET ALE HOUSE • CHICAGO
Punch, which is likely derived
from the Hindi word for "five," is
traditionally made with five
ingredients: liquor, sugar, citrus
juice, tea or spice and water.
The *Ti* in this traditional French-
Caribbean cocktail is short for
"petite," perhaps because the drink
has only four ingredients, or maybe
because it packs a small punch.

1 lime disk, cut from the side
  of a lime to include flesh, pith
  and skin (about ¼ inch thick)
1 teaspoon cane syrup, such as Depaz
1 cup crushed ice
2 ounces white rhum agricole
  (aromatic West Indian rum)

Working over a rocks glass, squeeze the
lime in both directions to squeeze the oil
and juice into the glass. Add the lime to
the glass along with the cane syrup and
half of the crushed ice. Set a long swizzle
stick or bar spoon in the glass and rub
it between your hands to mix the drink.
Add the rhum agricole and the remaining
crushed ice and mix again.

TI PUNCH
Clark Street Ale House, Chicago

Batida

SEVICHE • LOUISVILLE
Seviche chef and owner Anthony Lamas uses pure, naturally tart passion fruit juice in this spiked Brazilian drink. Passion fruit nectar, which is more widely available, makes a fine stand-in.

½ lime, cut into 6 small pieces
1 ounce Simple Syrup (p. 17)
Ice
1½ ounces cachaça (potent Brazilian sugarcane spirit)
1 ounce passion fruit nectar
½ ounce unsweetened coconut milk
½ ounce fresh lemon juice

In a cocktail shaker, muddle the lime and Simple Syrup. Add the remaining ingredients; shake well. Strain into an ice-filled rocks glass.

Marmalade Sour

VESSEL • SEATTLE
Mixologist Jamie Boudreau uses orange-and-grapefruit marmalade in his cachaça-based sour at Vessel.

2 ounces cachaça (potent Brazilian sugarcane spirit)
½ ounce fresh lemon juice
¼ ounce Simple Syrup (p. 17)
2 dashes of orange bitters
1 large egg white
1 tablespoon citrus marmalade
Ice

In a cocktail shaker, combine all of the ingredients except the ice. Shake well. Add ice; shake again. Strain into a chilled martini glass.

Caipirinha Manchada

ANDINA • **PORTLAND, OR**
Fruity *aguas frescas*, or "fresh waters," are popular all over Mexico. When head bartender Greg Hoitsma poured the purple-red Hibiscus Agua Fresca into this drink, he instantly came up with its name, which means "stained Caipirinha."

½ lime, cut into 6 pieces
¾ ounce Simple Syrup (p. 17)
1 cup ice
1½ ounces cachaça (potent Brazilian sugarcane spirit)
½ ounce Hibiscus Agua Fresca (below)

In a cocktail shaker, muddle the lime pieces with the Simple Syrup. Add the ice and cachaça and shake well. Pour into a rocks glass and pour the Hibiscus Agua Fresca over a bar spoon on top.

HIBISCUS AGUA FRESCA In a small heatproof bowl, steep 1 hibiscus tea bag in 8 ounces boiling water for 3 minutes. Remove the tea bag. Add 8 black peppercorns, ½ teaspoon cardamom and ¼ teaspoon each of allspice, cinnamon and cloves. Let cool. Strain the Hibiscus Agua Fresca through a coffee filter into an airtight container and refrigerate for up to 1 week. Makes 8 ounces.

PEPPER DELICIOUS, P. 84
Canlis, Seattle

Gin

James Bond Martini

SMOKY'S CLUB · MADISON, WI
For this variation on the Vesper from Ian Fleming's first James Bond novel, *Casino Royale,* bar manager "Martini Bob" Perry adds a Wisconsin touch: blue cheese–stuffed olives.

Ice
3 ounces gin
1 ounce vodka
½ ounce Lillet Blanc
3 blue cheese–stuffed olives, skewered on a pick

Fill a cocktail shaker with ice. Add the gin, vodka and Lillet Blanc. Shake well and strain into a chilled martini glass. Garnish with the stuffed olives.

Twelve-Dollar Martini

SAUCEBOX · PORTLAND, OR
Like the underground classic Dreamy Dorini Smoking Martini, this pleasantly smoky drink is tailor-made for cigar lovers. The name mocks inflated cocktail prices across the country.

½ ounce Pernod
Ice
3 ounces gin
¾ ounce dry vermouth
½ ounce Scotch, preferably Islay
1 lemon twist

Rinse a chilled martini glass with the Pernod, then pour it out. Fill a pint glass with ice. Add the gin, vermouth and Scotch. Stir well and strain into the prepared martini glass. Garnish with the lemon twist.

JAMES BOND MARTINI
Smoky's Club,
Madison, WI

Flower of My Secret

AMADA · PHILADELPHIA
All the cocktails at this Spanish tapas restaurant are named after Pedro Almodóvar films. In this case, the "secret" is rose-scented syrup.

One 3-inch piece of cucumber—
   peeled, seeded and diced,
   plus 1 cucumber wheel
½ ounce rose syrup
Ice
1½ ounces gin
½ ounce fresh lime juice
1 ounce chilled club soda

In a cocktail shaker, muddle the diced cucumber with the rose syrup. Add ice and the gin and lime juice. Shake well; strain into an ice-filled highball glass. Stir in the club soda; garnish with the cucumber wheel.

Sange du Nord

NO. 9 PARK · BOSTON
The bar team at No. 9 Park created this cocktail to promote the "Americans in Paris" exhibit at Boston's Museum of Fine Arts in 2006. The drink is a variation on the Monkey Gland, a classic cocktail made with Pernod: a perfect symbol of Paris.

Ice
2 ounces gin
1 ounce fresh orange juice
½ ounce Cointreau or other
   triple sec
¼ ounce Pernod

Fill a cocktail shaker with ice. Add all of the remaining ingredients and shake well. Strain into a chilled martini glass.

Basil Gimlet

THE HUNGRY CAT · LOS ANGELES

The Gimlet is named after British naval surgeon Sir Thomas Gimlette, who encouraged his shipmates to take their daily scurvy-fighting ration of preserved Rose's lime juice with gin, the staple spirit of the British Royal Navy.

Ice

2 ounces gin

¾ ounce fresh lime juice

1 ounce Basil Syrup (below)

1 basil leaf

Fill a cocktail shaker with ice. Add all of the remaining ingredients except the basil leaf. Shake well and strain into an ice-filled rocks glass. Garnish with the basil leaf.

BASIL SYRUP In a small saucepan, bring 6 ounces Simple Syrup (p. 17) to a boil. Remove from the heat and add 8 large basil leaves. Let cool, then refrigerate overnight. Strain the syrup into an airtight container and refrigerate for up to 3 weeks. Makes 6 ounces.

The Harrier

RESTAURANT EUGENE · ATLANTA
Mixologist Greg Best named his lavender-scented riff on a Greyhound—made with gin instead of vodka—after a dog known for its keen sense of smell: the harrier.

Ice
2 ounces gin
½ ounce Tincture of Lavender (below)
3 ounces fresh grapefruit juice
1 fresh lavender sprig

Fill a cocktail shaker with ice. Add all of the remaining ingredients except the lavender sprig. Shake well and strain into an ice-filled collins glass. Garnish with the lavender sprig.

TINCTURE OF LAVENDER In a small jar, combine 2½ ounces vodka with ¼ teaspoon dried lavender, cover tightly and store at room temperature for 1 week. Strain and store in the airtight container for up to 1 month. Makes about 2½ ounces.

THE HARRIER
Restaurant Eugene, Atlanta

Rush Street Highball

DAVID BURKE'S PRIMEHOUSE ·
CHICAGO

Mixologist and former molecular biologist Eben Klemm says, "I wanted to create a drink that achieved complexity not with weird ingredients but through the interplay between simple ones"—thyme, cranberries, apple juice and gin.

Ice

2 ounces gin

1 ounce chilled apple juice

¾ ounce fresh lemon juice

¾ ounce Simple Syrup (p. 17)

1 thyme sprig, plus 3 cranberries skewered on a pick

Fill a cocktail shaker with ice. Add the gin, apple and lemon juices and Simple Syrup. Shake well; strain into an ice-filled highball glass. Garnish with the thyme and cranberries.

Pepper Delicious

CANLIS · **SEATTLE**

Mixologist Ryan Magarian promises that the herby flavors of the gin combined with the mint and pepper in this drink will be a revelation for the non-gin drinker.

4 thin red bell pepper rings

7 mint leaves

1 ounce fresh lime juice

¾ ounce Simple Syrup (p. 17)

Ice

2 ounces gin

In a cocktail shaker, muddle 3 pepper rings with the mint, lime juice and Simple Syrup. Add ice and the gin; shake well. Strain into a chilled martini glass and garnish with the remaining pepper ring.

The Astoria Bianco

GRAMERCY TAVERN · NEW YORK CITY

This spin on the Astoria cocktail from Albert Stevens Crockett's *The Old Waldorf-Astoria Bar Book* substitutes a sweet bianco vermouth for a hard-to-find gin called Old Tom.

Ice

- 3 ounces gin
- 1 ounce bianco vermouth (sweet white vermouth)
- 2 dashes of orange bitters
- 1 orange twist

Fill a pint glass with ice. Add the gin, vermouth and orange bitters; stir well. Strain into a chilled coupe and garnish with the orange twist.

The Journalist

CORTEZ · SAN FRANCISCO

This drink appears in Harry Craddock's 1930 classic, *The Savoy Cocktail Book*. Craddock was a New York City bartender who traveled to London to work during Prohibition; his book was one of the first to include both European and American cocktails.

Ice

- 1½ ounces gin
- ¼ ounce sweet vermouth
- ¼ ounce dry vermouth
- ¼ ounce fresh lemon juice
- ¼ ounce Cointreau or other triple sec

Dash of Angostura bitters

- 1 lemon twist

Fill a cocktail shaker with ice. Add all of the remaining ingredients except the lemon twist. Shake well and strain into a chilled martini glass. Garnish with the lemon twist.

Blackbird

LANTERN • CHAPEL HILL, NC
"When I make my drinks, I look to the kitchen, particularly to the pastry chef," says bar manager Kristen Johnson. "The fruit and herbs that are at the farmers' market go into her desserts; those same things show up in my cocktails."

4   blackberries
4   lemon verbena leaves, plus 1 sprig
¾   ounce Simple Syrup (p. 17)
Ice
1½   ounces gin
½   ounce fresh lime juice
1   ounce chilled club soda

In a cocktail shaker, muddle the blackberries with the lemon verbena leaves and Simple Syrup. Add ice and the gin and lime juice. Shake well and strain into an ice-filled rocks glass. Stir in the club soda and garnish with the lemon verbena sprig.

Clover Club

DEVIN TAVERN • NEW YORK CITY
This cocktail was created in the late 19th century for a group of influential men who met at the bar of Philadelphia's old Bellevue-Stratford Hotel.

Ice
2   ounces gin
1   ounce fresh lemon juice
¾   ounce raspberry syrup

Fill a cocktail shaker with ice. Add all of the remaining ingredients. Shake well and strain into a chilled martini glass.

BLACKBIRD
Lantern, Chapel Hill, NC

Ramos Gin Fizz

THE ALEMBIC · SAN FRANCISCO

The original Ramos Gin Fizz served at Henry Ramos's famous late-19th-century New Orleans saloon was shaken for two minutes to thoroughly froth the egg white. Shaking egg white cocktails without ice, then shaking them again with ice emulsifies the white and adds an airy texture.

2 ounces gin

1 ounce Simple Syrup (p. 17)

½ ounce fresh lemon juice

½ ounce fresh lime juice

1 ounce heavy cream

1 large egg white

4 drops of orange flower water, such as A. Monteux

Ice

1 ounce chilled club soda

In a cocktail shaker, combine all of the ingredients except the ice and club soda. Shake vigorously for 30 seconds. Add ice, then shake again. Strain into a highball glass and pour in the club soda.

The Aviator

MARTINI MONKEY · **SAN JOSE, CA**

The Aviator is bar manager Jay Crabb's variation on the Aviation cocktail, which first appeared in Hugo Ensslin's 1916 book, *Recipes for Mixed Drinks*. Ensslin, the head bartender at the Wallick Hotel in New York City's Times Square, called for crème de violette, which gave the drink a sky-blue tinge.

1½ ounces gin
½ ounce maraschino liqueur
   (bittersweet cherry liqueur)
¾ ounce fresh lemon juice
½ ounce Simple Syrup (p. 17)
2 dashes of orange bitters
1 large egg white
Ice
½ ounce crème de cassis
   (black currant liqueur)

In a cocktail shaker, combine all of the ingredients except the ice and crème de cassis. Shake vigorously for 30 seconds. Add ice, then shake again. Strain into a chilled martini glass. Pour the crème de cassis on top of the drink.

Gin

Citron Shake

BRANDY LIBRARY • NEW YORK CITY
Brandy Library houses one of the
largest collections of spirits
(not just brandy) in the country.
Spirit sommelier Ethan Kelley
created this spin on the White
Lady cocktail that Harry
MacElhone served at Harry's
New York Bar in Paris in 1929. It
includes limoncello, a sweet,
lemon-flavored liqueur from Italy.

1½ ounces gin
¾ ounce limoncello
     (lemon-flavored liqueur)
½ ounce heavy cream
 1 large egg white
½ ounce Simple Syrup (p. 17)
Ice
½ teaspoon finely grated
     lemon zest

In a cocktail shaker, combine all
of the ingredients except the ice
and grated lemon zest. Shake
vigorously for 30 seconds. Add
ice, then shake again. Strain into a
chilled martini glass. Garnish with
the grated lemon zest.

CITRON SHAKE
Brandy Library,
New York City

Gin

Pastille

TRESTLE ON TENTH · NEW YORK CITY
Bartender Michael Reynolds's flowery variation on the Alaska cocktail, named after French pastille candy, complements chef Ralf Kuettel's hearty, Swiss-accented American cuisine.

½ ounce Pernod
Ice
3 ounces gin
¼ ounce green Chartreuse
10 drops of rose flower water

Rinse a chilled martini glass with the Pernod, then pour it out. Fill a pint glass with ice and add all of the remaining ingredients. Stir well and strain into the prepared martini glass.

Ginger Juice

BIN 8945 WINE BAR & BISTRO · WEST HOLLYWOOD
"Most of the drinks I make are froufrou," confesses bartender Damian Windsor. This one, made with a ginger-flavored liqueur, is an exception. "It's a masculine cocktail," he says. "The sherry makes it dry and the ginger gives it a lot of heat. Robert De Niro loves it."

1 teaspoon honey
Ice
3 ounces gin
1 ounce crème de gingembre, such as G.E. Massenez
1 ounce fino sherry
2 dashes of Angostura bitters

Drizzle the inner rim of a chilled martini glass with the honey. Fill a pint glass with ice. Add all of the remaining ingredients to the pint glass and stir well. Strain into the prepared martini glass.

Lychee & Lemongrass Fizz

FLATIRON LOUNGE · NEW YORK CITY

When Flatiron Lounge co-owner and mixologist Julie Reiner was growing up in Hawaii, she had a lychee tree in her backyard.

2 canned lychees, drained
½ ounce Lemongrass Syrup (below)
Ice
2 ounces gin
½ ounce fresh lime juice
1 ounce chilled club soda
1 fresh lemongrass stalk and
1 lime wheel

In a cocktail shaker, muddle the lychees with the Lemongrass Syrup. Add ice and the gin and lime juice. Shake well and strain into an ice-filled highball glass. Stir in the club soda and garnish with the lemongrass stalk and lime wheel.

LEMONGRASS SYRUP In a small saucepan, bring 6 ounces Simple Syrup (p. 17) to a boil. Remove from the heat and add 1 coarsely chopped stalk of fresh lemongrass. Let cool, then refrigerate overnight. Strain the syrup into an airtight container and refrigerate for up to 3 weeks. Makes 6 ounces.

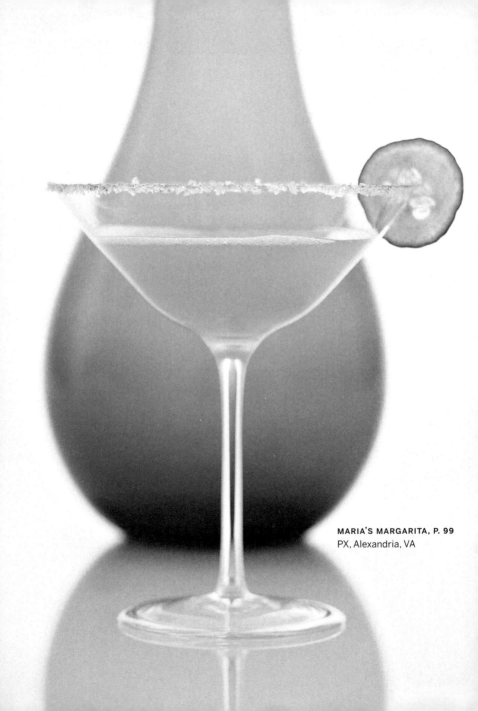

MARIA'S MARGARITA, P. 99
PX, Alexandria, VA

Tequila

Prickly Pear

MADURO • MADISON, WI
Bartender Brook Chisholm named this cocktail after the cacti that often grow near agave, the plant used to make tequila. According to owner Brian Haltinner, "We have six types of bitters, but good old Angostura gives the best prickle."

Ice

2 ounces silver tequila

1 ounce pear liqueur, such as Mathilde

¾ ounce fresh lime juice

Dash of Angostura bitters

1 prickly pear or pear slice and 2 lime wheels

Fill a cocktail shaker with ice. Add all of the remaining ingredients except the prickly pear and lime wheels; shake well. Strain into an ice-filled highball glass; garnish with the prickly pear and lime wheels.

Tequila Smash

GRAMERCY TAVERN • NEW YORK CITY
Bartender Jim Meehan, the deputy editor of this book, created this cocktail for "Taste of the Nation," a fundraiser that helps feed hungry children in the U.S.

4 blueberries

4 brandied cherries

½ cup ice

2 ounces silver tequila

½ ounce maraschino liqueur (bittersweet cherry liqueur)

½ ounce fresh lime juice

In a cocktail shaker, muddle the berries and cherries. Add the ice, tequila, maraschino liqueur and lime juice. Shake well and pour into a rocks glass.

PRICKLY PEAR
Maduro, Madison, WI

Tequila Sunset

PARK PLACE ON MAIN • LOUISVILLE
Former general manager Jerry Slater uses Chambord instead of grenadine to create the brilliant colors in this riff on a Tequila Sunrise. Cocktail historians Dave Wondrich and Steven Olson trace the Tequila Sunrise back to the end of Prohibition at Tijuana's famed Agua Caliente resort-racetrack.

¾ ounce honey
Ice
1½ ounces silver tequila
½ ounce fresh orange juice
½ ounce fresh lemon juice
¼ ounce Chambord

Drizzle the honey around the inner rim of a chilled martini glass. Fill a cocktail shaker with ice. Add the tequila and citrus juices; shake well. strain into the prepared martini glass. Pour the Chambord over the drink.

Azteca

TRECE • DALLAS
Chef Amador Mora fashioned this drink after a traditional Mexican tequila cocktail that a friend from the Yucatán shared with him one Christmas.

Ice
3 ounces silver tequila
1 ounce pineapple juice
1 ounce fresh grapefruit juice
½ ounce almond syrup
1 lime wheel

Fill a cocktail shaker with ice. Add all of the remaining ingredients except the lime wheel. Shake well and strain into an ice-filled highball glass. Garnish with the lime wheel.

Maria's Margarita

PX • ALEXANDRIA, VA
Mixologist Todd Thrasher created this margarita to entice his wife into visiting him at PX, the 1920s-style speakeasy above the restaurant Eamonn's: A Dublin Chipper. The margarita's flavors are based on a spicy Salvadoran chile mix she likes to sprinkle on cucumbers.

1 lime wedge and spice mix
  (1 teaspoon each of superfine sugar, cayenne pepper and sea salt)
2 Cucumber Ice Cubes (below)
2 ounces silver tequila
1 ounce Cointreau or other triple sec
1 ounce Cucumber Mix (below)
1 cucumber wheel

Moisten the outer rim of a martini glass with the lime wedge and coat lightly with the spice mix. Put the Cucumber Ice Cubes in a cocktail shaker. Add the tequila, Cointreau and Cucumber Mix. Shake well and strain into the prepared martini glass. Garnish with the cucumber wheel.

CUCUMBER ICE CUBES & CUCUMBER MIX
In a medium bowl, mix the juice of 2 English cucumbers with 2½ ounces fresh lemon juice, 2½ ounces fresh lime juice, ½ teaspoon salt and ¾ ounce Simple Syrup (p. 17). Pour into an ice cube tray and freeze; reserve the remaining Cucumber Mix for the drink. Makes 1 dozen ice cubes and 8 ounces Cucumber Mix.

Tequila

L'il Jig

PEGU CLUB • NEW YORK CITY
Bartender Phil Ward named this herbaceous variation on a margarita after the smaller of two jiggers that Pegu Club staffers use to pour each drink precisely.

3   Thai basil leaves
¾   ounce fresh lime juice
½   ounce Simple Syrup (p. 17)
Ice
1½ ounces silver tequila
½   ounce yellow Chartreuse

In a cocktail shaker, muddle the basil leaves with the lime juice and Simple Syrup. Add ice and the tequila and Chartreuse. Shake well and strain into a chilled coupe.

La Melonada

LAS PALMAS • CHICAGO
La Melonada is based on a traditional Mexican *agua fresca*—made with fruit, herbs, spices and water. The usual garnish at Las Palmas: skewered cantaloupe balls.

¾   cup cantaloupe cubes
One ½-inch piece of peeled fresh ginger, chopped
2   ounces silver tequila
¾   ounce Cointreau or other triple sec
½   ounce water
¾   ounce Simple Syrup (p. 17)
¾   ounce fresh lime juice
Ice

In a blender, puree all of the ingredients except the ice. Strain into an ice-filled shaker. Shake well; strain into a chilled martini glass.

L'IL JIG
Pegu Club, New York City

Mexican Café Martini

MASA • MINNEAPOLIS
As the base for this cool and creamy cocktail, bar manager Rebecca Habeck uses *café de olla,* a Mexican spiced coffee named after the earthenware pot in which it's traditionally prepared.

Ice
1½ ounces silver tequila
1½ ounces chilled Spiced Coffee (below)
½ ounce coffee liqueur, such as Tia Maria
½ ounce heavy cream
3 coffee beans

Fill a cocktail shaker with ice. Add all of the remaining ingredients except the coffee beans. Shake well and strain into a chilled martini glass. Garnish with the coffee beans.

SPICED COFFEE In a coffee press or heatproof pitcher, combine ⅔ cup ground coffee beans, 1 tablespoon each of ground cinnamon and dark brown sugar, 1 teaspoon each of grated nutmeg and ground cloves and four 2-by-½-inch strips of orange zest. Cover with 4 cups boiling water. Let steep for 4 minutes. Plunge the coffee or strain it through a coffee filter into an airtight container and refrigerate for up to 1 day. Makes 32 ounces.

Bridget's Strawberry Margarita

TWO • SAN FRANCISCO
At Two, the new, laid-back reincarnation of owner David Gingrass's beloved Hawthorne Lane, the cocktails are prepared with house-made infusions and squeezed-to-order fruit juices.

5 lemon wedges and superfine sugar
1 ounce Simple Syrup (p. 17)
Ice
2 ounces Strawberry Tequila (below)
1 ounce Cointreau or other triple sec
1 strawberry

Moisten the outer rim of a martini glass with 1 lemon wedge and coat lightly with sugar. In a cocktail shaker, muddle the 4 remaining lemon wedges with the Simple Syrup. Add ice and the Strawberry Tequila and Cointreau. Shake well and strain into the prepared martini glass. Garnish with the strawberry.

STRAWBERRY TEQUILA Quarter 1 pint of strawberries. In an airtight container, cover the strawberries with one 750-ml bottle of reposado tequila and refrigerate overnight. Strain the tequila through a coffee filter and refrigerate in an airtight container for up to 1 week. Makes about 25 ounces.

Agave Negro

SOCIAL HOLLYWOOD ·
LOS ANGELES

Beverage director and sommelier Franklin Ferguson's inspiration for this drink was bubble tea. The round sections of blackberry (called drupelets) mimic the look of the tapioca pearls in the popular Asian beverage.

2 blackberries, plus 1 blackberry and 1 lime wheel skewered on a pick
1 cup ice
1½ ounces reposado tequila
¾ ounce fresh lime juice
¾ ounce Simple Syrup (p. 17)
½ ounce Chambord
1 ounce chilled club soda

In a cocktail shaker, muddle the 2 blackberries. Add the ice, tequila, lime juice, Simple Syrup and Chambord. Shake well and pour into a rocks glass. Stir in the club soda and garnish with the skewered blackberry and lime wheel.

AGAVE NEGRO
Social Hollywood, Los Angeles

Smooth & Tropical

WATERSTREET CAFÉ & BAR ·
OLYMPIA, WA

Former Waterstreet bar manager Justin Hosford says he made this drink for two reasons. "One, I always try to have a drink that people find slightly strange on my cocktail menu. If anything, it creates conversation. Two, I don't keep a blender behind my bar, so I wanted to create a drink with a naturally smooth texture."

3 lime wedges
1 thick avocado wedge
1 tablespoon raspberry preserves
Ice
1½ ounces reposado tequila
¾ ounce Cointreau or other triple sec
2 ounces pear nectar
1 ounce fresh grapefruit juice

In a cocktail shaker, muddle 2 lime wedges with the avocado wedge and raspberry preserves. Add ice and the tequila, Cointreau, pear nectar and grapefruit juice. Shake well and strain into a chilled martini glass. Garnish with the remaining lime wedge.

Mexico City

TRES AGAVES · SAN FRANCISCO
Bartender Jacques Bezuidenhout invented this drink as a way to feature oaky añejo tequila. Cherry Heering, a Danish liqueur made with cherry brandy, balances the woody flavor.

Ice
- 2 ounces añejo tequila
- ½ ounce sweet vermouth
- ½ ounce Cherry Heering or cherry liqueur
- 3 brandied cherries, skewered on a pick

Fill a pint glass with ice. Add the tequila, vermouth and Cherry Heering. Stir well and strain into a chilled coupe. Garnish with the skewered cherries.

Nouveau Carré

ABSINTHE BRASSERIE & BAR · SAN FRANCISCO
This riff on the classic rye-based Vieux Carré cocktail is mixologist Jonny Raglin's tribute to New Orleans: "I chose an aged tequila to replace the rye because it has a spicy backbone that can stand up to the sweet Bénédictine and Lillet."

Ice
- 1½ ounces añejo tequila
- ¾ ounce Bénédictine (golden herbal liqueur)
- ¼ ounce Lillet Blanc
- 5 dashes of Peychaud's bitters
- 1 lemon twist

Fill a pint glass with ice. Add all of the remaining ingredients except the lemon twist and stir well. Strain into a chilled coupe and garnish with the lemon twist.

DRY COUNTY COCKTAIL (LEFT), P. 115
Absinthe Brasserie & Bar, San Francisco
AQUEDUCT, P. 111
Thoroughbred Club, Charleston, SC

Whiskey

Whiskey

Marmalade Whiskey Sour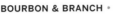

BOURBON & BRANCH ·
SAN FRANCISCO
Bourbon & Branch refers to a simple cocktail made with bourbon and branch water, a term first used in the 1800s to refer to pure, clean water from a tiny stream called a branch.

Ice
2½ ounces bourbon
1 ounce fresh lemon juice
¾ ounce Simple Syrup (p. 17)
1 teaspoon orange marmalade
1 dash of orange bitters
1 orange twist

Fill a cocktail shaker with ice. Add all of the remaining ingredients except the orange twist and shake vigorously for 30 seconds to dissolve the marmalade. Strain into a chilled martini glass. Garnish with the orange twist.

Manhattan via Jerez

TORO · **BOSTON**
When Adam St. Jean interviewed for the bartender position at the tapas restaurant Toro, he created this drink to complement the menu. It's a Manhattan that substitutes the sweet, raisiny Spanish sherry Pedro Ximénez for vermouth.

Ice
3 ounces bourbon
½ ounce Pedro Ximénez sherry
2 to 3 dashes of Angostura bitters
3 brandied cherries, skewered on a pick

Fill a pint glass with ice. Add the bourbon, sherry and bitters and stir well. Strain into a chilled coupe and garnish with the skewered cherries.

Aqueduct

**THOROUGHBRED CLUB •
CHARLESTON, SC**
Many of the cocktails at the
Thoroughbred Club are named
after racetracks or horse-
racing terms. This variation on
the old-fashioned is named
after the one racetrack located
within New York City limits.

2 maraschino cherries, plus
1 maraschino cherry and
1 orange wheel skewered
on a pick
1 orange slice, halved crosswise
¼ ounce Simple Syrup (p. 17)
2 dashes of Angostura bitters
2 ounces bourbon
Ice
1 ounce chilled club soda

In a rocks glass, muddle the
2 cherries with the orange slice,
Simple Syrup and bitters.
Add the bourbon, then fill the
glass with ice and add the club
soda. Pour the drink back and
forth between the rocks glass
and a pint glass 3 times, then pour
it into the rocks glass. Garnish
with the skewered cherry and
orange wheel.

The Charleston Bog

INDIGO LANDING · ALEXANDRIA, VA
With Indigo Landing's low-country menu in mind, mixologist Ralph Rosenberg wanted to create a bourbon drink that was appealing to non-bourbon drinkers. The result, which Rosenberg makes with Maker's Mark bourbon, is this lightly sweet pink drink.

4 raspberries
8 mint leaves, plus 1 mint sprig
2 lime wedges
½ ounce Honey Syrup (below)
Ice
3 ounces bourbon
1 ounce white cranberry juice

In a cocktail shaker, muddle the raspberries with the mint leaves, lime wedges and Honey Syrup. Add ice and the bourbon and cranberry juice. Shake well and strain into a pilsner glass. Garnish with the mint sprig.

HONEY SYRUP In a small heatproof bowl, stir 1 cup honey with ½ cup boiling water until dissolved. Let cool, then refrigerate in an airtight container for up to 1 month. Makes 12 ounces.

THE CHARLESTON BOG
Indigo Landing, Alexandria, VA

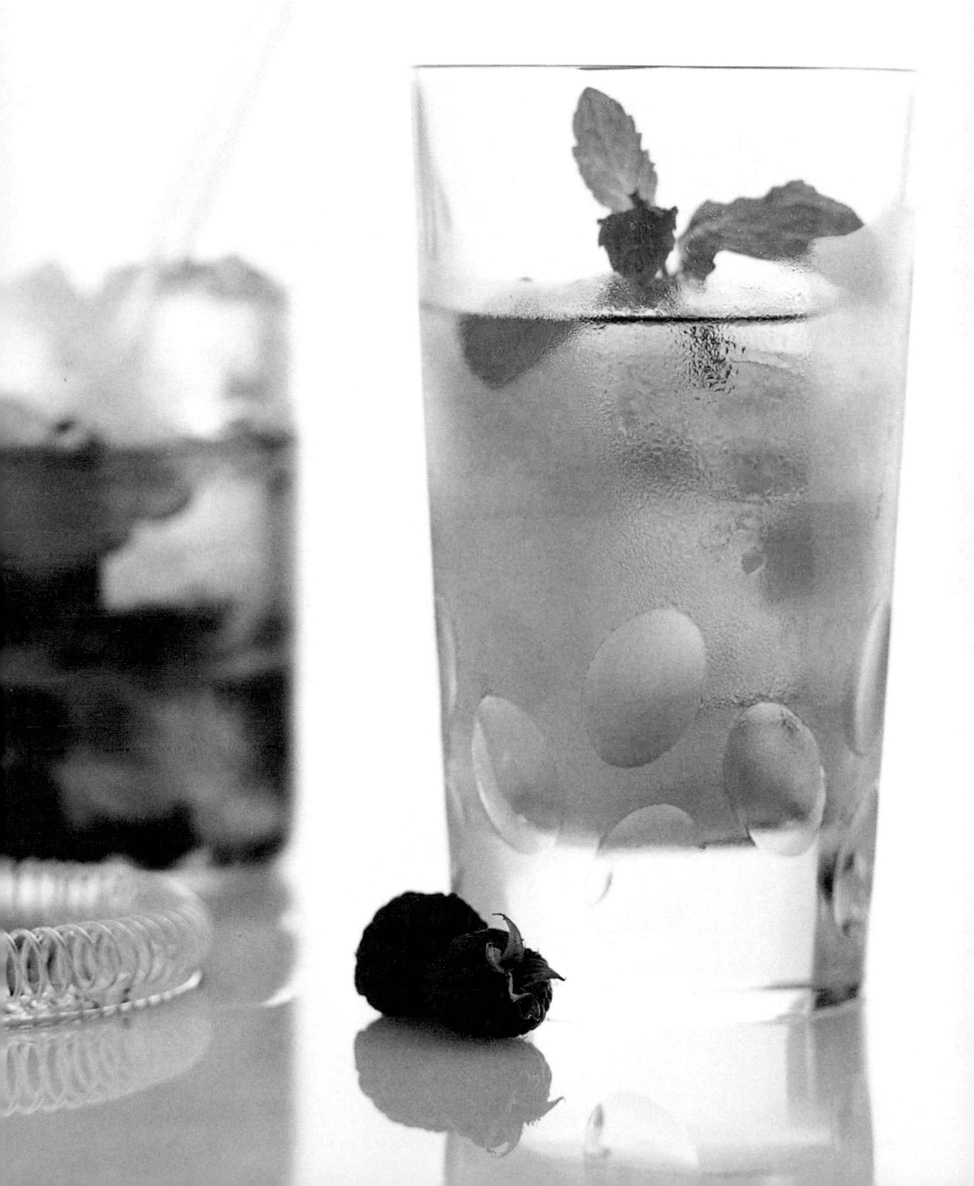

Weeski

5 NINTH • NEW YORK CITY
Mixologist Dave Wondrich wanted to make Manhattans for some friends but all he had in his liquor cabinet that even came close to the necessary ingredients (vermouth and rye) was Irish whiskey and Lillet Blanc— and so the Weeski was born.

Ice

2 ounces Irish whiskey
1 ounce Lillet Blanc
¾ ounce Cointreau or other triple sec
2 dashes of orange bitters
1 orange twist

Fill a pint glass with ice. Add all of the remaining ingredients except the orange twist and stir well. Strain into a chilled coupe and garnish with the orange twist.

The Hazlewood

HAZLEWOOD • SEATTLE
Ex-Soundgarden bassist Ben Shepherd and Droo Church bassist-bartender Drew Church named their turn-of-the-century-style lounge after Lee Hazlewood, a 1960s and '70s singer, songwriter and record producer.

Ice

3 ounces Irish whiskey
½ ounce Amaretto
2 ounces chilled strong peppermint tea
1 lemon twist

Fill a cocktail shaker with ice. Add the whiskey, Amaretto and peppermint tea and shake well. Strain into a chilled martini glass and garnish with the lemon twist.

Dry County Cocktail

ABSINTHE BRASSERIE & BAR ·
SAN FRANCISCO
This drink's name is a nod to the whiskey that bartender Jonny Raglin uses in it: Jack Daniel's, which is distilled in the dry county of Moore, Tennessee.

Ice
2   ounces Tennessee whiskey
¾   ounce dry vermouth
½   ounce Ginger Syrup (p. 64)
1   dash of lemon bitters
1   lemon twist

Fill a pint glass with ice. Add all of the remaining ingredients except the lemon twist and stir well. Strain into a chilled coupe. Flame the lemon twist over the drink (p. 121), then drop it in.

Indian Summer

FREEMANS · NEW YORK CITY
Co-owner William Tigertt uses vanilla-spiced bianco vermouth in his low-proof spin on a dry Manhattan.

Ice
1½   ounces bourbon
1½   ounces bianco vermouth
      (sweet white vermouth)
1   lemon twist

Fill a pint glass with ice. Add the bourbon and vermouth and stir well. Strain into a chilled coupe and garnish with the lemon twist.

Kentucky Cousin

TOWN TALK DINER · MINNEAPOLIS
Not all of the drinks at this
newly renovated 1940s diner
have risqué names, but, says
bar manager Nick Kosevich,
"It's great when a 60-year-old
lady orders a Panty Dropper."

4 mint leaves, plus
   1 mint sprig
3 lemon slices
4 brandied cherries
½ ounce Simple Syrup (p. 17)
1 cup ice
2 ounces bourbon
½ ounce Cherry Heering or
   cherry liqueur
1 ounce chilled brewed black tea
½ ounce fresh lemon juice

In a cocktail shaker, muddle the mint
leaves with 2 lemon slices, 3 cherries
and the Simple Syrup. Add the ice,
bourbon, Cherry Heering, tea and lemon
juice. Shake well and pour into a rocks
glass. Garnish with the mint sprig and
remaining lemon slice and cherry.

KENTUCKY COUSIN
Town Talk Diner, Minneapolis

Clermont Smash

BOA STEAKHOUSE · LAS VEGAS
Smashes are drinks traditionally made with a spirit and crushed ice, flavored with mint and dressed with any variety of seasonal fruit. Tony Abou-Ganim's variation is named after Clermont, Kentucky, where the Beam family distillery reopened after Prohibition ended in 1934.

10 to 12 mint leaves, plus
    1 mint sprig
¾ ounce Velvet Falernum
    (clove-spiced liqueur)
Ice cubes, plus crushed ice
1½ ounces bourbon
1 ounce fresh lemon juice
3 dashes of peach bitters
1 pineapple spear

In a cocktail shaker, muddle the mint leaves with the Velvet Falernum. Add ice cubes and the bourbon, lemon juice and bitters and shake well. Strain into a rocks glass filled with crushed ice and stir until the outside of the glass begins to frost. Rub the rim of the glass with the pineapple spear, then garnish with the pineapple spear and mint sprig.

Man of Leisure

JACK THE HORSE TAVERN · BROOKLYN, NY

Mixologist Damon Dyer based this drink on a mid-20th-century cocktail named for the famous racehorse Man o' War, replacing the orange curaçao in the original with pear flavored Belle de Brillet.

Ice
1½ ounces bourbon
½ ounce Belle de Brillet or pear liqueur
½ ounce Cointreau or other triple sec
½ ounce sweet vermouth
½ ounce fresh lemon juice
Dash of Angostura bitters

Fill a cocktail shaker with ice. Add all of the remaining ingredients and shake well. Strain into a chilled martini glass.

Winged Victory

ASPEN · NEW YORK CITY

Holly Roberts's drink is named after the white-marble statue of the Greek goddess of victory, Nike. In certain light, the statue can appear almost copper in tone, just like this cocktail.

Ice
2½ ounces bourbon
1½ ounces chocolate liqueur
¾ ounce amontillado sherry
3 coffee beans

Fill a pint glass with ice. Add the bourbon, chocolate liqueur and sherry and stir well. Strain into a chilled coupe and garnish with the coffee beans.

Sazerac

THE MOTEL BAR · CHICAGO

The modern Sazerac has rye whiskey as its base, but this version hearkens back to the original Sazerac, which was made with Cognac and served at New Orleans's Sazerac Coffee House.

½ ounce Pernod
1 sugar cube
3 dashes of Peychaud's bitters
2 dashes of Angostura bitters
Ice
1½ ounces Cognac
1½ ounces rye
1 lemon twist

Rinse a chilled rocks glass with the Pernod, then pour it out. In a cocktail shaker, muddle the sugar cube with both bitters. Add ice and the Cognac and rye and stir until the sugar is nearly dissolved, about 40 seconds. Strain into the prepared rocks glass. Twist the lemon twist over the drink and then discard it.

CITRUS TWIST BASICS A twist adds concentrated citrus flavor from the peel's essential oils. To make a twist, cut a piece of the peel (avoiding the white pith) into a 1½-by-½-inch strip. Twist or squeeze the strip, rub the zest around the rim of the glass, then drop it into the drink or discard it.

Sherman's Revenge

TROIS · ATLANTA

After a stint in New York City, mixologist Eric Simpkins returned home to invigorate the Atlanta cocktail scene with this allusion to the rebuilding of the city after Union General Sherman set it on fire during the Civil War.

2½	ounces rye
1	ounce cream sherry
1	dash of orange bitters
3	orange twists
Ice	

In a pint glass, combine the rye, sherry and bitters. Flame 2 orange twists (below) over the glass, then drop them into it. Add ice and stir well. Strain into a chilled coupe. Flame the remaining twist over the drink, then drop it in.

FLAMING A TWIST Flaming a lemon or orange twist caramelizes and enriches the zest's essential oils. Start by cutting a thin, oval, quarter-size piece of zest with a bit of the white pith intact. Grasping the outer edges gently between the thumb, middle and index fingers, hold the twist, skin side down, about 4 inches over the cocktail. Hold a lit match an inch away from the twist, then pinch the edges sharply together to propel the citrus oil through the flame and into the drink.

Whiskey

Ruby Tuesday

EMPLOYEES ONLY · NEW YORK CITY
On a quiet Tuesday afternoon, co-owner Dushan Zaric muddled cherries with rye and Bénédictine to create this drink. "The whole cocktail was conceived and mixed while the Rolling Stones's 'Ruby Tuesday' was playing; coincidentally, the cocktail has a ruby-red color," says Zaric.

4 brandied cherries
¾ ounce fresh lemon juice
½ ounce Simple Syrup (p. 17)
Ice
1½ ounces rye
¾ ounce Bénédictine
(brandy-based herbal liqueur)
1 lemon twist

In a cocktail shaker, muddle the cherries with the lemon juice and Simple Syrup. Add ice and the rye and Bénédictine. Shake well and strain into a chilled martini glass. Garnish with the lemon twist.

Little Italy

PEGU CLUB · NEW YORK CITY
Mixologist Audrey Saunders uses the Italian artichoke liqueur Cynar to accent the vermouth in this tribute to the famous Manhattan neighborhood Little Italy.

Ice
2 ounces rye
½ ounce Cynar (artichoke liqueur)
¾ ounce sweet vermouth
2 maraschino cherries, skewered on a pick

Fill a pint glass with ice. Add the rye, Cynar and vermouth and stir vigorously. Strain into a chilled coupe. Garnish with the skewered cherries.

Green Velvet

MICHAEL MINA · SAN FRANCISCO
Besides having composed one of the best—and at 2,600 bottles, biggest—wine lists in San Francisco, acclaimed wine director Rajat Parr also creates unusual drinks like this spicy rye cocktail.

Ice
3 ounces rye
2 dashes of orange bitters
¾ ounce Punt e Mes (bittersweet vermouth)
¾ ounce yellow Chartreuse
1 orange twist

Fill a pint glass with ice. Add all of the remaining ingredients except the twist; stir well. Strain into a chilled coupe. Flame the twist over the drink (p. 121), then drop it in.

Copper Swan

LUCQUES · LOS ANGELES
This cocktail pays homage to the swan-necked copper pot stills traditionally used to produce Scottish whisky. Fruit preserves are substituted for the apricot brandy in the original.

Ice
1½ ounces Highland single-malt Scotch
½ ounce sweet vermouth
½ ounce fresh lemon juice
1 tablespoon apricot preserves
2 dashes of Peychaud's bitters
1 orange twist

Fill a cocktail shaker with ice. Add all of the remaining ingredients except the twist. Shake well and strain into a chilled martini glass. Garnish with the twist.

APPLE BOMB, P. 132
Rye, San Francisco

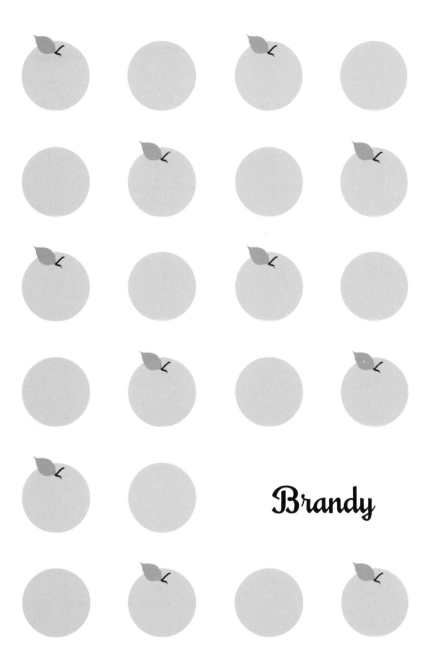

Brandy

American Beauty

BLUE DUCK TAVERN ·
WASHINGTON, DC

This classic cocktail was
likely named after
Washington, DC's official
flower, the American
Beauty Rose, because of
the drink's blush color.

Ice

1½ ounces Cognac
¼ ounce crème de menthe
¼ ounce Simple Syrup (p. 17)
1 ounce fresh orange juice
½ ounce grenadine
¼ ounce tawny port
1 mint sprig

Fill a cocktail shaker with ice. Add all
of the remaining ingredients except
the port and mint. Shake well; strain
into a chilled martini glass. Stir
in the port. Garnish with the mint.

Between the Sheets

BIN 54 · **CHAPEL HILL, NC**

Although a recipe for
Between the Sheets
appeared in 1930's *The
Savoy Cocktail Book*,
Prohibition-era bartender
Johnny Brooks claims
authorship of the recipe
in his 1954 book, *My
35 Years Behind Bars*.

Ice

¾ ounce gin
¾ ounce Cointreau or other triple sec
¾ ounce Cognac
¼ ounce fresh lemon juice
1 lemon twist

Fill a cocktail shaker with ice. Add
all of the remaining ingredients
except the lemon twist. Shake well
and strain into a chilled martini
glass. Garnish with the lemon twist.

AMERICAN BEAUTY
Blue Duck Tavern, Washington, DC

Lemon Zest 🍸

BALEEN SAN DIEGO · SAN DIEGO

Palo cortado is a special variety of sherry that's known for having both the rich, nutty flavor of an oloroso and the bright acidity of an amontillado. Mixologist Brian Van Flandern blends it with gin and Cognac in this spin on a Collins.

Ice

- 1 ounce Cognac
- ¾ ounce palo cortado or amontillado sherry
- ½ ounce gin
- 1 ounce fresh lemon juice
- ½ ounce Simple Syrup (p. 17)
- 1 ounce chilled lemon soda
- 1 lemon twist

Fill a cocktail shaker with ice. Add all of the remaining ingredients except the lemon soda and lemon twist. Shake well and strain into a chilled martini glass. Stir in the lemon soda. Flame the twist over the drink (p. 121), then drop it in.

Astolfi

JACK'S LA JOLLA · SAN DIEGO
Bill Berkley named his
17,500-square-foot, four-
level restaurant after
his 91-year-old father, Jack.
Later, Berkley's wife and
daughters realized that
it was also an acronym for
their names: Jenny,
Allison, Connie and Kelly.

Ice
1½ ounces Cognac
1½ ounces Cointreau or other triple sec
 1 ounce pineapple juice
Dash of Angostura bitters
Pinch of freshly grated nutmeg and
     1 orange twist

Fill a cocktail shaker with ice. Add
the Cognac, Cointreau, pineapple
juice and bitters; shake well. Strain
into a chilled martini glass. Garnish
with the nutmeg and the twist.

White Star Imperial Daisy

5 NINTH · NEW YORK CITY
This drink is named after the
White Star cruise ships that
docked at the turn of the
20th century at the piers near
where 5 Ninth is located.

Ice
 2 ounces Armagnac
 ½ ounce kümmel (liqueur flavored
     with cumin, caraway and fennel)
 ½ ounce fresh lemon juice
 1 teaspoon cane syrup, such as Depaz
 1 ounce Champagne

Fill a cocktail shaker with ice. Add all
of the remaining ingredients except
the Champagne. Shake well and
strain into a chilled coupe. Stir in the
Champagne.

Brandy

Somerset Sidecar

PLUCKEMIN INN • BEDMINSTER, NJ

Bar manager Tad Carducci was inspired to create this holiday sidecar by the bowls of apples, oranges and nuts that his mom sets out around the house before Christmas.

1 lemon wedge and Hazelnut Sugar (below)

Ice

1½ ounces apple brandy

¾ ounce Cointreau or other triple sec

¾ ounce fresh lemon juice

½ ounce Frangelico

1 orange twist

Moisten the outer rim of a martini glass with the lemon wedge and coat lightly with the Hazelnut Sugar. Fill a cocktail shaker with ice. Add the apple brandy, Cointreau, lemon juice and Frangelico. Shake well and strain into the prepared glass. Garnish with the orange twist.

HAZELNUT SUGAR In a mini food processor, pulse ⅓ cup toasted skinned hazelnuts with ¼ cup superfine sugar until sandy with some slightly larger bits. Store in an airtight container at room temperature for up to 1 week. Makes about ½ cup.

SOMERSET SIDECAR
Pluckemin Inn, Bedminster, NJ

Brandy

Apple Bomb

RYE · SAN FRANCISCO

This drink was created on New Year's Day 2006 as part of a special menu called "Healthy Hair of the Dog Cocktails."

Ice

2 ounces applejack
2 ounces chilled apple juice
1½ ounces chilled ginger beer
3 pieces of candied ginger or 1 apple slice, skewered on a pick

Fill a cocktail shaker with ice. Add the applejack and apple juice and shake well. Stir in the ginger beer and strain into an ice-filled rocks glass. Garnish with the candied ginger.

Bonds's Cocktail No. 1

MOXIE · CHICAGO

This drink is the first of a series of cocktails named after baseball legend Barry Bonds, who shares a birthday with mixologist John Kinder.

Ice

2 ounces Calvados
½ ounce Honey Syrup (p. 112)
¾ ounce Lillet Blanc
2 dashes of peach bitters

Fill a pint glass with ice. Add all of the remaining ingredients. Stir well and strain into a chilled coupe.

Sideways Sour

CUBA LIBRE · PHILADELPHIA
This unorthodox take on a
Pisco Sour gets finished
with a shot of Pinot Noir.

1½ ounces pisco (South American
    grape-based spirit)
½ ounce Cointreau or other triple sec
1½ ounces chilled white grape juice
½ ounce fresh lemon juice
½ ounce fresh lime juice
1 large egg white
Ice
½ ounce Pinot Noir

In a cocktail shaker, combine all of the
ingredients except the ice and Pinot
Noir. Shake vigorously for 30 seconds.
Add ice and shake again. Strain into a
chilled martini glass. Add the Pinot Noir.

Casanova

PROVIDENCE · LOS ANGELES
Mixologist Vincenzo Marianella
named this smooth grappa
cocktail after the 18th-century
Venetian playboy Casanova.

Ice
2 ounces grappa
½ ounce Licor 43 (sweet citrus-
    and vanilla-flavored liqueur)
1 ounce fresh lemon juice
½ ounce Simple Syrup (p. 17)
½ ounce tawny port

Fill a cocktail shaker with ice. Add all
of the remaining ingredients. Shake well
and strain into a chilled martini glass.

TALL NAPOLEON, P. 138
Bistro Vendôme, Denver

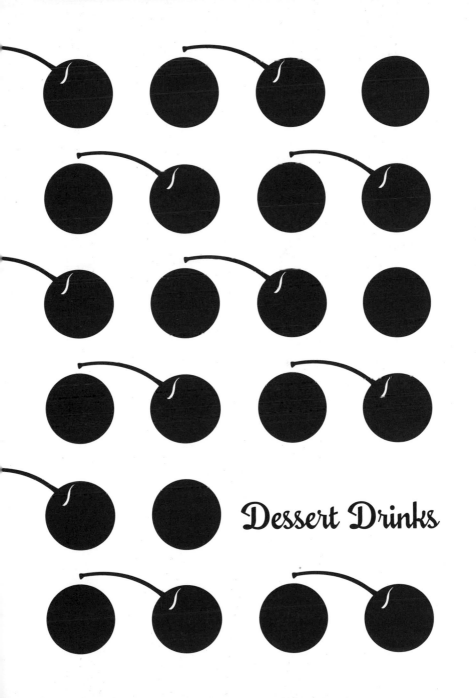

Dessert Drinks

Dessert Drinks

Chocolate-Raspberry Truffletini

CAROUSEL LOUNGE • NEW ORLEANS
"This is like a really fine chocolate truffle that melts in your mouth," says bartender Marvin Allen. He makes this variation on a chocolate martini with nocino, a walnut liqueur produced in Modena, Italy.

Ice
2 ounces vanilla vodka
1 ounce Irish cream
¾ ounce Chambord
¾ ounce coffee liqueur
½ ounce walnut liqueur
Chocolate shavings and 2 raspberries

Fill a cocktail shaker with ice. Add all of the remaining ingredients except the chocolate shavings and berries; shake well. Strain into a chilled martini glass. Garnish with the chocolate and berries.

Count Strega

ARNAUD'S FRENCH 75 BAR • NEW ORLEANS
Bartender Chris Hannah and Cocktaildb.com guru Ted Haigh were bemoaning how few drinks are made with the saffron-colored herbal liqueur Strega ("witch" in Italian), so Hannah created one.

1 strawberry, plus 1 strawberry slice
Ice
1½ ounces Strega (herbal liqueur)
1½ ounces tawny port
4 dashes of Peychaud's bitters

In a pint glass, muddle the strawberry. Add ice and the Strega, port and bitters; stir well. Strain into a chilled martini glass. Garnish with the strawberry slice.

**CHOCOLATE-RASPBERRY
TRUFFLETINI**
Carousel Lounge,
New Orleans

Chai Latte

TORNADO STEAK HOUSE •
MADISON, WI
General manager Mel
Trudeau and bar manager
Rick Vanderheite infuse
vodka and other spirits with
fruit, herbs and spices
to create seasonal cocktails
like this wintry variation
on a White Russian.

Ice
3 ounces Chai Vodka (below)
1 ounce heavy cream
¾ ounce Simple Syrup (p. 17)
¼ ounce dark-chocolate liqueur

Fill a cocktail shaker with ice. Add the
Chai Vodka, cream and Simple Syrup.
Shake well and strain into a chilled
martini glass. Drizzle the chocolate
liqueur on top.

CHAI VODKA In a jar, combine 8 ounces
vodka with 2 tablespoons loose chai tea.
Let stand at room temperature for 45
minutes. Strain through a coffee filter
into an airtight container; refrigerate
for up to 3 weeks. Makes 8 ounces.

Tall Napoleon

BISTRO VENDÔME • DENVER
This cocktail is a pousse-café, a
multicolored drink made by
layering liqueurs on top of each
other, with the heaviest spirit
on the bottom and the least
dense, and strongest, on top.

1 ounce chilled Bénédictine
   (brandy-based herbal liqueur)
1 ounce chilled green Chartreuse
1 ounce chilled Cognac

Pour the Bénédictine over a bar spoon
into a cordial glass. Repeat with the
Chartreuse and Cognac.

Brandy Milk Punch

**OLD ABSINTHE HOUSE •
NEW ORLEANS**
This drink is a house favorite at the Old Absinthe House, which is located in New Orleans's French Quarter in a building that became a saloon in 1815.

Ice
2 ounces whole milk
1½ ounces brandy
½ ounce Simple Syrup (p. 17)
4 drops of pure vanilla extract
Pinch of freshly grated nutmeg

Fill a cocktail shaker with ice. Add all of the remaining ingredients except the nutmeg. Shake well and strain into an ice-filled rocks glass. Garnish with the nutmeg.

Spanish Alexander

ROUX • PORTLAND, OR
Roux's drink menu is organized into sections like "the Quarter" (New Orleans classics), "the Garden District" (drinks with "a touch more sophistication") and "the Bayou" (spicy cocktails and rich nightcaps like this creamy concoction).

Ice
¾ ounce brandy
¾ ounce Tia Maria (coffee liqueur)
¾ ounce Licor 43 (sweet citrus- and vanilla-flavored liqueur)
¼ ounce heavy cream
Pinch of ground cinnamon

Fill a cocktail shaker with ice. Add all of the remaining ingredients except the cinnamon. Shake well and strain into a chilled martini glass. Garnish with the cinnamon.

Dessert Drinks

Chartreuse Swizzle

HARRY DENTON'S STARLIGHT ROOM • SAN FRANCISCO Marco Dionysos, one of the many talented mixologists at Harry Denton's, entered this drink in a Bay Area cocktail competition—and won.

Ice cubes, plus shaved ice
1¼ ounces green Chartreuse
½ ounce Velvet Falernum (clove-spiced liqueur)
1 ounce pineapple juice
½ ounce fresh lime juice
1 lime wheel or 1 pineapple spear

Fill a cocktail shaker with ice cubes. Add the Chartreuse, Velvet Falernum and fruit juices; shake well. Strain into a rocks glass filled with shaved ice. Garnish with the lime wheel.

Snowstorm Café

39 DEGREES • ASPEN Bartender Denis Côté created this drink as a warmer-upper for guests who've just returned from skiing or snowboarding on Aspen Mountain, which is right outside the lounge.

3 ounces hot strong-brewed coffee
1 ounce Frangelico
½ ounce Licor 43 (sweet citrus- and vanilla-flavored liqueur) or Navan
½ ounce Cognac
1 large dollop of unsweetened whipped cream
3 coffee beans

In a mug, mix the coffee with the Frangelico, Licor 43 and Cognac. Top with the whipped cream and garnish with the coffee beans.

SNOWSTORM CAFÉ (LEFT)
39 Degrees, Aspen
CHAI LATTE, P. 138
Tornado Steak House, Madison, WI

Dessert Drinks

Martinique Apple Pie ▼

TAILOR • NEW YORK CITY
At dessert specialist Sam Mason's brand-new restaurant Tailor, he collaborated with mixologist Eben Freeman on the cocktail list. They make the Brown Butter Rum by adding rum to browned butter, cooling the mixture and discarding the solid butter from the infused spirit. Mason and Freeman use a similar technique with spices, olive oil and even bacon fat.

Honey and 1 graham cracker, finely crushed
Ice
2½ ounces Brown Butter Rum (below)
1½ ounces chilled apple cider
Pinch of freshly grated nutmeg

Moisten the outer rim of a martini glass with honey and coat lightly with the graham cracker crumbs. Freeze until firm. Fill a cocktail shaker with ice. Add the Brown Butter Rum and apple cider. Shake well and strain into the martini glass. Garnish with the nutmeg.

BROWN BUTTER RUM In a small saucepan, cook 4 tablespoons unsalted butter, stirring, until nut-brown. Pour into a heatproof bowl and stir in 5 ounces rhum agricole (aromatic West Indian rum). Cover and refrigerate overnight. Break the butter layer and pour the rum through a fine strainer into an airtight container. Refrigerate for up to 3 days. Makes about 5 ounces.

Hot Buttered Rum

CYRUS • HEALDSBURG, CA
For this drink and many of his other seasonal creations, bar manager Scott Beattie prefers to use Charbay vanilla rum, one of the many artisanal spirits now produced in California.

2 ounces melted Spiced Vanilla
  Ice Cream (below)
2 ounces boiling water
1½ ounces vanilla-spiced rum
Pinch of freshly grated nutmeg

In a mug, mix the Spiced Vanilla Ice Cream with the boiling water and rum. Garnish with the nutmeg.

SPICED VANILLA ICE CREAM In a medium saucepan, combine 1 cup vanilla ice cream, 4 tablespoons unsalted butter, 4 ounces heavy cream, 1 tablespoon each of granulated sugar and dark brown sugar and ⅛ teaspoon each of ground cinnamon, ground allspice and freshly grated nutmeg and bring to boil. Cook, stirring frequently, until the sugars are dissolved, about 2 minutes. Remove from the heat and let cool. Refrigerate for up to 4 days; reheat before using. Makes about 14 ounces.

WATERMELON SANGRIA, P. 152
Del Toro Café y Taberna, Chicago

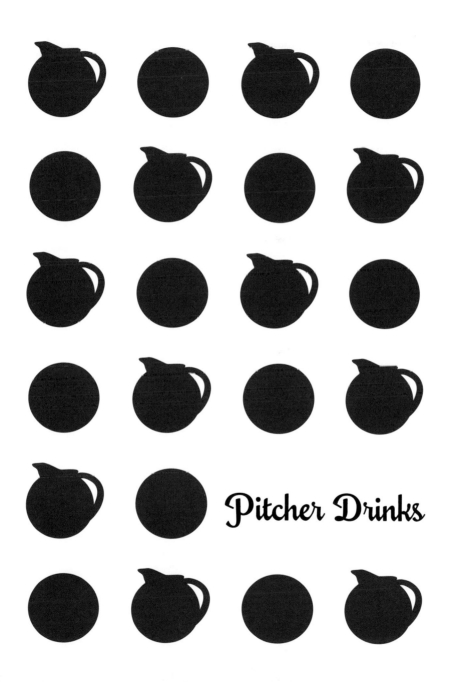

Pitcher Drinks

Limoncello Collins

HATFIELD'S • LOS ANGELES
The Collins was most likely named after 19th-century bartender John Collins of London's Limmer's Hotel. The Tom Collins was originally made with Old Tom, a sweet style of gin that's extremely hard to find today.

MAKES 8 DRINKS

16 ounces limoncello
(lemon-flavored liqueur)
12 ounces gin
8 ounces fresh lemon juice
24 paper-thin lemon slices
Ice
16 ounces chilled club soda
8 mint sprigs

In a pitcher, combine the limoncello, gin and lemon juice. Cover and refrigerate until chilled, at least 2 hours. Press 3 thin lemon slices against the inside of each of 8 collins glasses. Add ice to the glasses. Stir the limoncello mixture and pour it into the glasses. Stir 2 ounces club soda into each drink and garnish with a mint sprig.

LIMONCELLO COLLINS
Hatfield's, Los Angeles

Small Batch Gin & Tonic

PARK KITCHEN • PORTLAND, OR
Bartender Tim Ludwig
is less than thrilled about
the sweet, artificially
flavored tonic water that's
commercially available, so
he did some research and
created his own Tonic Syrup,
which he adds to club soda.

MAKES 8 DRINKS

12 ounces gin
4 ounces Tonic Syrup (below)
Ice
16 ounces chilled club soda
8 lime wedges

In a pitcher, combine the gin
and Tonic Syrup. Cover and
refrigerate until chilled, at least
2 hours. Stir and pour into 8 ice-
filled highball glasses. Top each
drink with 2 ounces club soda
and stir, then garnish with a
lime wedge.

TONIC SYRUP In a small
saucepan, bring 1 cup water
to a boil. Stir in 1 cup sugar,
1 lime half, 2 coarsely chopped
fresh lemongrass stalks,
½ teaspoon ground cinchona
bark (p. 215) and 1 teaspoon
citric acid powder (p. 215).
Simmer over moderate heat
for 15 minutes. Strain through
a coffee filter into an airtight
container and refrigerate for
up to 3 weeks. Makes about
12 ounces.

Triestine Iced Tea

FRASCA FOOD & WINE •
BOULDER, CO
On an annual staff trip to
Friuli, Italy, the Frasca
employees discovered
Cynar, a bitter liqueur made
from 13 herbs and plants,
including the artichoke
(Cynara scolymus). Adding
limoncello and club soda
dilutes Cynar's intense
flavor and gives the drink
an iced-tea color.

MAKES 8 DRINKS

16 ounces Cynar (artichoke liqueur)
8 ounces limoncello
    (lemon-flavored liqueur)
Ice
20 ounces chilled club soda
8 lemon wedges

In a pitcher, combine the Cynar
and limoncello. Cover and
refrigerate until chilled, at least
2 hours. Stir the mixture and pour
into 8 ice-filled collins glasses.
Top each drink with 2½ ounces
club soda and stir, then garnish
with a lemon wedge.

Zee Spotted Pig Bloody Mary

THE SPOTTED PIG • NEW YORK CITY
Bartender Anna Vanderzee suggests making the mix for this recipe one day in advance to allow the spices and horseradish to marry with the tomato juice.

MAKES 8 DRINKS

½ cup finely grated peeled fresh horseradish

2 ounces Worcestershire sauce

2 ounces Sriracha chile sauce

Finely grated zest of 1 small lemon

2 teaspoons celery salt

1 teaspoon kosher salt

Freshly ground pepper

32 ounces tomato juice

Ice

16 ounces vodka

Lime wedges and pickled or fresh vegetables (optional)

1. In a pitcher, combine the horseradish, Worcestershire sauce, Sriracha, lemon zest, celery salt, kosher salt and 2 teaspoons ground pepper. Add the tomato juice and stir well. Cover and refrigerate until chilled, at least 2 hours.

2. Pour the tomato juice mixture into 8 ice-filled rocks glasses. Add 2 ounces vodka to each glass and stir. Garnish each drink with a pinch of ground pepper, a lime wedge and pickled vegetables.

ZEE SPOTTED PIG BLOODY MARY
The Spotted Pig, New York City

Watermelon Sangria

**DEL TORO CAFÉ Y TABERNA •
CHICAGO**
Sangria, a Spanish variation on traditional punch composed of wine, fruit and brandy, was formally introduced to America at the 1964 World's Fair in New York City. Del Toro Café features classic Spanish sangria alongside seasonal versions such as this recipe, which chef Andrew Zimmerman created for the summer with vodka instead of brandy.

MAKES 6 TO 8 DRINKS

2 pounds seedless watermelon, peeled and cubed, plus ½ pound watermelon cut into balls with a melon baller and skewered on picks
1 bottle dry white wine
6 ounces vodka
4 ounces Cointreau or other triple sec
4 ounces Citrus Syrup (below)
Ice

In a blender, puree the watermelon cubes. Pour through a fine strainer into a pitcher. Add the white wine, vodka, Cointreau and Citrus Syrup. Stir and refrigerate for at least 2 hours. Stir again, then pour the sangria into ice-filled white wine glasses and garnish with the skewered watermelon balls.

CITRUS SYRUP In a small saucepan, bring 6 ounces Simple Syrup (p. 17) to a boil. Remove from the heat and add one 2-inch lemon zest strip and one 2-inch orange zest strip. Let cool, then refrigerate overnight. Strain the syrup into an airtight container and refrigerate for up to 3 weeks. Makes 6 ounces.

Jala-piña

PROOF ON MAIN • LOUISVILLE
Cocktail consultant Rob Larcom uses fresh pineapple juice, which isn't as cloying as the canned version, to sweeten a traditional margarita, and then spices it up with jalapeño pepper.

MAKES 8 DRINKS

- ½ ripe pineapple, peeled and cut into large chunks
- 17 ounces silver tequila
- 2 ounces fresh lime juice
- ¼ cup sugar
- 1 small jalapeño, seeded and finely chopped

Ice

- 8 pineapple wedges

Working in batches in a blender, puree the pineapple chunks with the tequila. Transfer to a large airtight container and stir in the lime juice, sugar and jalapeño. Cover and refrigerate overnight. Strain the pineapple-infused tequila; stir well. Pour into 8 ice-filled rocks glasses and garnish with the pineapple wedges.

Pitcher Drinks

La Real

**SOLSTICE RESTAURANT & LOUNGE •
SAN FRANCISCO**

The "La" in this drink's name references La Pinta pomegranate tequila; the "Real," which means "royal" in Spanish, refers to the sparkling wine in the blend (as in a Kir Royale). You can substitute the more available Pama liqueur when La Pinta isn't available.

MAKES 8 DRINKS

8 ounces silver tequila
8 ounces pomegranate liqueur
4 ounces Cointreau or other triple sec
24 ounces chilled brut sparkling wine
8 thin orange twists

In a pitcher, combine the tequila, pomegranate liqueur and Cointreau. Cover and refrigerate until chilled. Stir and pour into 8 chilled flutes. Pour 3 ounces sparkling wine into each drink and garnish with a twist.

Dubious Manhattan

BOKA KITCHEN & BAR • SEATTLE

Dubonnet red is a wine-based aperitif with a bittersweet flavor that comes from quinine, an extract of the cinchona tree bark that has been used as a healthy additive to fortified wines for centuries.

MAKES 6 DRINKS

4 ounces Dubonnet red
4 ounces sweet vermouth
16 ounces bourbon
¼ ounce peach bitters
18 brandied cherries, skewered on 6 picks

In a pitcher, combine the Dubonnet red, sweet vermouth, bourbon and peach bitters. Cover and refrigerate until chilled, at least 2 hours. Stir and pour into 6 chilled coupes. Garnish with the skewered cherries.

Royal Fruit Cup

THE SLANTED DOOR •
SAN FRANCISCO
This drink is an approximation
of the original Pimm's
No. 1 Cup, a recipe invented in
the 1840s by James Pimm,
who became famous for the
bottled cocktails he sold
at his oyster bar in London.

MAKES 8 DRINKS

16 ounces House Fruit Cup (below)
2 ounces fresh lemon juice
Ice
8 ounces chilled ginger beer
24 ounces chilled sparkling wine
8 Thai basil sprigs, 8 orange twists
and 8 cucumber spears (optional)

In a pitcher, combine the House
Fruit Cup and lemon juice. Cover
and refrigerate until chilled, at
least 2 hours. Stir and pour into
8 ice-filled pilsner glasses. Stir
1 ounce ginger beer and 3 ounces
sparkling wine into each drink and
garnish with a basil sprig, orange
twist and cucumber spear.

HOUSE FRUIT CUP In an airtight
container, combine 4 ounces each
of gin, Campari, dry vermouth
and sweet vermouth, preferably
Carpano Antica Formula.
Refrigerate for up to 2 months.
Makes 16 ounces.

PEACHY SWEET, P. 158
Eleven, West Hollywood

Virgin Cocktails

Virgin Cocktails

Mango Lassi

TABLA · NEW YORK CITY

In India, a traditional *lassi* is made by blending yogurt with water, salt and spices until frothy. This fruity version is a perfect match for chef Floyd Cardoz's Indian-spiced food.

Ice
- 3 ounces plain whole milk yogurt
- 3 ounces mango nectar
- 1 ounce whole milk
- ½ to 1 ounce Simple Syrup (p. 17)

Ground cumin

Fill a cocktail shaker with ice. Add all of the remaining ingredients except the cumin. Shake well and strain into an iced-filled pilsner glass. Top with a dusting of cumin.

Peachy Sweet

ELEVEN · WEST HOLLYWOOD

Co-owner Sid Krofft, who produced numerous 1970s television series including *The Bugaloos* and *Land of the Lost*, employed lighting designers, stage producers and choreographers to create this entertainment-meets-dining spectacle. The name refers to the hour at which Eleven transforms from restaurant to nightclub.

- 2 ounces peach nectar
- 1 ounce chilled apple juice

Four ½-inch-thick banana slices
- 1 ounce sweetened coconut milk
- 1 ounce whole milk
- ½ cup crushed ice
- 3 very thin coconut slices or 1 peach slice

In a blender, combine all of the ingredients except the coconut slices. Puree until smooth. Pour into a chilled highball glass and garnish with the coconut slices.

Hibiscus Cooler

FARMER BROWN · SAN FRANCISCO
Chef-owner Jay Foster combined citrus and pineapple juices with tea made from dried Jamaican hibiscus flowers to create this vitamin C–rich drink.

Ice

8 ounces chilled brewed hibiscus tea
1 ounce Simple Syrup (p. 17)
¾ ounce pineapple juice
½ ounce fresh lime juice
½ ounce fresh orange juice
1 thin strawberry slice

Fill a pilsner glass with ice. Add all of the remaining ingredients except the strawberry slice and stir. Float the strawberry slice on the surface of the drink.

New Orleans Buck

FLATIRON LOUNGE · NEW YORK CITY
Traditionally, a buck— lemon or lime juice, a spirit and ginger ale—would be served in a tall glass with a citrus wedge or twist. The Flatiron Lounge lists this nonalcoholic version on its extensive mocktail menu.

Ice

1½ ounces pineapple juice
¾ ounce fresh lime juice
2 ounces chilled ginger beer
1 piece of candied ginger and 1 lime wheel

Fill a highball glass with ice. Add the pineapple juice, lime juice and ginger beer and stir. Garnish with the candied ginger and lime wheel.

Virgin Cocktails

Strawberry Lemonade

PARLOR • CHICAGO

This drink was originally part of a "Think Pink" menu that raised money for a local breast cancer charity.

2 large strawberries

Ice

3 ounces fresh lemon juice

1½ ounces water

1½ ounces Simple Syrup (p. 17)

2 lemon wedges

In a cocktail shaker, muddle the strawberries. Add ice and the lemon juice, water and Simple Syrup. Shake well and strain into an ice-filled highball glass. Garnish with the lemon wedges.

Green Tea Press

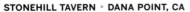

STONEHILL TAVERN • DANA POINT, CA

General manager Tim Flowers based Stonehill Tavern's entire drink list on classic cocktails. To make this alcohol-free sparkler, he replaces the bourbon in a Presbyterian with organic Cloud Mist green tea.

Ice

2 ounces chilled brewed green tea

1 ounce Ginger Syrup (p. 64)

2 ounces chilled club soda

1 lime wedge and 1 mint sprig

Fill a pint glass with ice. Add the green tea, Ginger Syrup and club soda and stir well. Pour into a highball glass and garnish with the lime wedge and mint sprig.

STRAWBERRY LEMONADE
Parlor, Chicago

Tuscan Fresco

BOKA KITCHEN & BAR • SEATTLE

"A lot of restaurants treat virgin cocktails like vegetarian dishes: They just make a drink from the regular menu and leave out the alcohol," says executive chef Seis Kamimura. "I love the challenge of creating original nonalcoholic drinks that are special in their own right."

Ice

2 rosemary sprigs
1 ounce peach nectar
1 ounce white cranberry juice
½ ounce fresh lemon juice
½ ounce Simple Syrup (p. 17)
1 ounce chilled club soda

Fill a cocktail shaker with ice. Add 1 rosemary sprig and the peach nectar, white cranberry juice, lemon juice and Simple Syrup. Shake well and strain into an ice-filled rocks glass. Stir in the club soda and garnish with the remaining rosemary sprig.

TUSCAN FRESCO
BOKA Kitchen & Bar, Seattle

Virgin Bellini

DEL POSTO • NEW YORK CITY
Hard cider was a staple
beverage in America until
Prohibition, when producers
cut down their cider apple
trees to grow sweet apples.

Ice

1 ounce Strawberry Puree (below)
4 ounces chilled sparkling apple
   cider
1 strawberry slice

Fill a pint glass with ice. Add the
Strawberry Puree and cider. Stir
well and strain into a chilled flute.
Garnish with the strawberry slice.

STRAWBERRY PUREE Halve 1 pint
of stawberries. In a medium
saucepan, combine the halved
strawberries with ¼ cup sugar
and 6 tablespoons water and bring
to a boil, stirring to dissolve the
sugar. Let cool, then add ¾ ounce
fresh lemon juice. Transfer to a
blender and puree until smooth.
Pour the puree through a fine
strainer into an airtight container
and refrigerate for up to 3 days.
Makes about 12 ounces.

Roe's Virgin Cocktail

THE STANTON SOCIAL · **NEW YORK CITY**
Co-owner Peter Kane created this drink for his wife, who wasn't drinking alcohol at the time. "I wanted it to be a cocktail that would make her feel like she was a having a real night out."

8 mint leaves
2 clementine wedges
Ice
2 ounces fresh tangerine juice
½ ounce fresh lime juice
½ ounce Simple Syrup (p. 17)
1 ounce chilled club soda

In a cocktail shaker, muddle the mint leaves with the clementine wedges. Add ice, the tangerine and lime juices and the Simple Syrup. Shake well and strain into an ice-filled highball glass. Stir in the club soda.

My Thai

NORA'S CUISINE · **LAS VEGAS**
Mixologist Cameron Bogue's inspiration for this mocktail came from a salad of green papaya, melon and Thai basil he ate during a trip to southern Thailand.

5 Thai basil leaves, plus 1 Thai basil sprig
¾ ounce demerara sugar
2 ounces fresh honeydew juice
Ice
3 cantaloupe balls
1½ ounces chilled club soda

In a pint glass, muddle the basil leaves and demerara sugar with the honeydew juice. Strain into a collins glass and add ice and the cantaloupe balls. Stir in the club soda; garnish with the basil sprig.

LOBSTER SLIDERS, P. 176
28 Degrees, Boston

Bar Food

Caramel Corn

PS 7'S · WASHINGTON, DC

Chef-owner Peter Smith's sweet, hazelnut-flecked popcorn is a riff on the bowls of nuts and popcorn that line so many bars.

8 SERVINGS

10 cups lightly salted plain popped popcorn

½ cup blanched hazelnuts, toasted and chopped

½ cup dark brown sugar

¼ cup light corn syrup

2 tablespoons unsalted butter

1 teaspoon pure vanilla extract

½ teaspoon kosher salt

¼ teaspoon baking soda

Vegetable oil spray

1. Preheat the oven to 350°. Line a large rimmed baking sheet with a silicone liner or buttered parchment paper. In a large bowl, mix the popcorn and chopped nuts. In a small saucepan, combine the sugar, corn syrup and butter and bring to a boil. Cook over moderately high heat for 2 minutes. Off the heat, whisk in the vanilla, salt and baking soda. Immediately pour the caramel over the popcorn and toss with a rubber spatula coated with vegetable oil spray.

2. Spread the popcorn on the baking sheet and bake for 2 minutes; stir to coat. Repeat 3 more times, until the popcorn is evenly coated with caramel. Remove from the oven and stir until the caramel hardens, 5 minutes. Transfer to a bowl and serve.

CARAMEL CORN
PS 7's, Washington, DC

Spiced Almonds

NACIONAL 27 • CHICAGO

"I love all almonds but I'm *in love* with marcona almonds," says chef Randy Zweiban. At the restaurant, he cold-smokes the buttery Spanish almonds, then roasts them with a mix of smoky spices.

6 TO 8 SERVINGS

½ teaspoon ground cumin
½ teaspoon sugar
½ teaspoon freshly ground pepper
¼ teaspoon ground coriander
¼ teaspoon ancho chile powder
¼ teaspoon Pimentón de la Vera (smoked Spanish paprika)
¼ teaspoon kosher salt
½ pound marcona almonds

Preheat the oven to 350°. In a medium bowl, mix the cumin with the sugar, pepper, coriander, chile powder, smoked paprika and salt. Add the almonds and toss to coat with the spice mixture. Spread the almonds on a rimmed baking sheet and bake for about 8 minutes, stirring halfway through baking, until lightly toasted. Serve warm or at room temperature.

MAKE AHEAD The toasted almonds can be kept in an airtight container for up to 3 days.

Crispy Stuffed Olives

BB'S · CHICAGO

Chef Jerry Pelikan's reasons for creating this snack are hard to argue with. "People love olives and people love sausage," he says. "And since it's an appetizer, it had to be deep-fried." The dish is so popular that BB's goes through eight gallons of olives each week.

6 TO 8 SERVINGS

- 24 colossal green or black pitted olives (7½ ounces)
- 6 ounces spicy Italian sausage, cut into 24 pieces
- 30 saltine crackers
- 2 large eggs
- ½ cup skim milk
- ½ cup all-purpose flour

Vegetable oil, for frying

Lemon wedges, for serving

1. Cut a lengthwise slit down one side of each olive. Stuff a piece of Italian sausage into each olive.

2. In a food processor, pulse the crackers until finely ground. Transfer to a shallow bowl. In another shallow bowl, whisk the eggs with the milk. Put the flour in a third shallow bowl. Dredge the olives in the flour, then roll them in the eggs and finally in the cracker crumbs, tossing to coat thoroughly.

3. In a large saucepan, heat 1½ inches of vegetable oil to 325° over moderately high heat. Fry the olives, in batches, until golden brown, about 4 minutes. Transfer the olives to paper towels to drain. Serve hot with lemon wedges.

Bar Food

Chickpea Fries

PARK KITCHEN • PORTLAND, OR

At this excellent little restaurant, Scott Dolich (a FOOD & WINE Magazine Best New Chef 2004) serves these crisp-outside-tender-inside jumbo fries with homemade pumpkin ketchup, but they're also wonderful on their own. He spikes the fries with *sambal oelek*, a bright red Southeast Asian chile sauce available at Asian markets.

6 TO 8 SERVINGS

- 2 tablespoons extra-virgin olive oil
- 1 small onion, minced
- 4 garlic cloves, minced
- 1 teaspoon minced fresh rosemary
- 1½ teaspoons *sambal oelek*
- 4 cups water
- 2 cups chickpea flour
- Kosher salt
- Vegetable oil, for frying
- All-purpose flour, for dusting

1. Lightly oil a 9-by-13-inch baking pan. Heat the olive oil in a large saucepan. Add the onion, garlic and rosemary and cook over moderate heat until the onion is very tender, 6 minutes. Stir in the *sambal oelek*. Add the water and bring to a boil. Slowly whisk in the chickpea flour until smooth. Reduce the heat to low and whisk until very thick, about 6 minutes. Season with salt. Spread evenly in the oiled baking pan and press plastic wrap on the surface. Refrigerate until firm, at least 4 hours.

2. In a large pot, heat 2 inches of oil to 350°. Cut the chickpea mixture into 4-by-¾-inch fries and pat dry with paper towels. Lightly dust the fries with flour. Fry in batches until golden, 8 minutes. Drain on paper towels, season with salt and serve.

CHICKPEA FRIES
Park Kitchen, Portland, OR

Devils on Horseback

FREEMANS • NEW YORK CITY
The quirky menu at this hard-to-find yet wildly popular restaurant and bar includes this very classic British appetizer; it's a variation on Angels on Horseback, which is made with oysters instead of prunes and so-named because the cooked oyster edges resemble wings.

6 SERVINGS

20 pitted prunes
1½ ounces blue cheese, cut into 20 small pieces (about ⅓ cup)
10 slices of bacon (about 11 ounces), halved crosswise

Preheat the oven to 500°. Line a rimmed baking sheet with foil. Put the prunes in a medium bowl, cover with warm water and let plump for 15 minutes; drain and pat dry. Press a piece of blue cheese into the center of each prune. Wrap each prune with a bacon slice, making sure to cover the hole in the prune; secure each one with a toothpick. Arrange the prunes on the prepared baking sheet and bake for about 10 minutes, turning once, until the bacon is crisp. Drain on paper towels. Let stand for 5 minutes before serving.

Warm Piquillo & Crab Dip

AMADA · PHILADELPHIA

Chef Jose Garces offers a mix of traditional and inspired tapas at his terrific spot in Old City. This creamy pepper and seafood dip is a simplified version of the stuffed piquillo peppers on his menu.

6 TO 8 SERVINGS

- 1 pound lump crabmeat, picked over
- ¼ cup mayonnaise
- ¼ cup crème fraîche
- 2 tablespoons chopped flat-leaf parsley
- 2 tablespoons snipped chives
- 1 tablespoon Dijon mustard
- 2 teaspoons fresh lemon juice
- ¼ pound Manchego cheese, shredded (1 cup)

One 9-ounce jar piquillo peppers, drained and cut into strips

Crusty bread or crackers, for serving

Preheat the broiler. In a bowl, combine the crabmeat, mayonnaise, crème fraîche, parsley, chives, mustard, lemon juice and ¾ cup of the Manchego. Spread in an 8-by-11-inch baking dish. Top with the piquillos and sprinkle with the remaining Manchego. Broil until the cheese is melted and the dip is heated through. Serve hot with bread or crackers.

Lobster Sliders

28 DEGREES • BOSTON
These lush, miniature takes on classic New England lobster rolls are a staple of this sleek South End lounge and restaurant, one of the few places in Boston that serves great food late at night.

8 SERVINGS

Meat from a 1½-pound cooked lobster
   (1¼ cups), cut into ½-inch pieces
2 tablespoons mayonnaise
2 tablespoons crème fraîche
1 tablespoon minced shallot
1 tablespoon finely diced dill pickle
2 tablespoons finely diced celery
1½ teaspoons minced tarragon
½ teaspoon finely grated lemon zest
Kosher salt and freshly ground white pepper
1 tablespoon unsalted butter, at room
   temperature
Eight 2-inch round soft dinner rolls, split

1. In a medium bowl, mix the lobster with the mayonnaise, crème fraîche, shallot, pickle, celery, tarragon and lemon zest. Season with salt and white pepper and refrigerate until ready to use.

2. Lightly butter the cut side of each roll. Heat a large skillet over moderate heat. Toast the rolls in the skillet, cut side down, until lightly golden, about 1 minute. Transfer the rolls to a work surface. Spoon about 3 tablespoons of the lobster salad on the bottom half of each roll. Close the sliders and serve.

Spicy Glazed Shrimp

BIN 8945 WINE BAR & BISTRO ·
LOS ANGELES

These shrimp, which are coated in a fiery butter sauce, are based on a dish that chef Matt Carpenter encountered at cook shacks along the beach in Jamaica's Montego Bay. The surprise ingredient is ketchup, which is often used in Caribbean cooking.

8 SERVINGS

2 sticks unsalted butter, melted
1 tablespoon chopped fresh ginger
¼ cup ketchup
¼ cup white wine vinegar
3 tablespoons rice vinegar
2 tablespoons soy sauce
1¼ teaspoons cayenne pepper
1 teaspoon Pimentón de la Vera (smoked Spanish paprika)
Kosher salt and freshly ground pepper
2½ pounds large shrimp, peeled and deveined
2 tablespoons extra-virgin olive oil
1 baguette, sliced

1. In a blender, combine the melted butter with the ginger, ketchup, white wine vinegar, rice vinegar, soy sauce, cayenne and smoked paprika; blend until smooth. Transfer the butter sauce to a medium bowl and season with salt and pepper.

2. Season the shrimp with salt and pepper. In a very large skillet, heat the oil. Add the shrimp and cook over moderate heat, turning, until just white throughout, about 5 minutes. Remove the pan from the heat, add the butter sauce and toss to coat the shrimp. Transfer the shrimp to a bowl and serve hot with the bread.

Hot Wings

THE GOOD FORK • BROOKLYN, NY
The wonderfully spicy
chicken wings that husband-
and-wife owners Ben
Schneider and Sohui Kim
serve at their intimate,
Asian-inflected restaurant
are made with the popular
Thai chile sauce Sriracha
in place of the classic
Frank's Red Hot sauce; the
soothing accompaniment
is a mix of sour cream
spiked with rice vinegar.

6 SERVINGS

- 1 cup sour cream
- ¼ cup plus 1 tablespoon rice vinegar
- 3 scallions, white and tender green parts only, thinly sliced

Kosher salt and freshly ground pepper

- 1 cup Sriracha chile sauce
- 1 tablespoon *sambal oelek* or other Asian chile sauce
- 1 stick cold unsalted butter, cut into 8 pieces

Vegetable oil, for frying

- 3 pounds chicken wings, tips discarded, wings cut in half at the joint

1. In a bowl, mix the sour cream with 2 tablespoons of the rice vinegar and the scallions. Season with salt and pepper. Cover and refrigerate.

2. In a saucepan, combine the Sriracha, *sambal oelek* and the remaining 3 tablespoons of rice vinegar and bring to a boil. Remove from the heat and whisk in the butter until melted; keep warm.

3. In a large pot, heat 2 inches of oil to 375°. Pat the wings dry and fry in batches until crisp and cooked through, about 5 minutes. Drain on paper towels and season with salt and pepper. Transfer to a large bowl. Pour the hot chile sauce over the wings and toss to coat. Serve with the dipping sauce.

HOT WINGS
The Good Fork, Brooklyn, NY

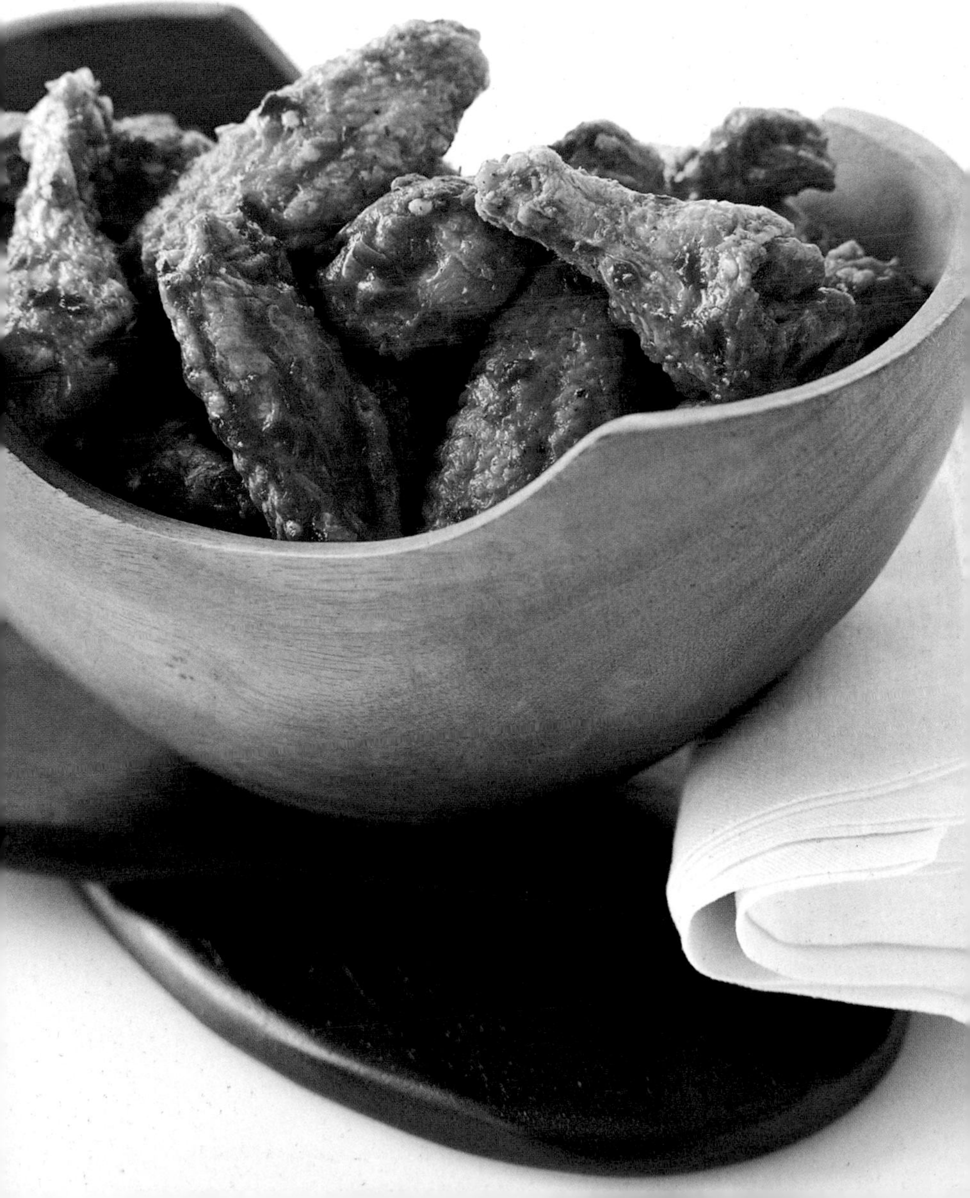

Steak Tartare

CUT • BEVERLY HILLS

At Beverly Hills's celebrated new steak house, Cut, chef Lee Hefter (a FOOD & WINE Magazine Best New Chef 1998) makes his over-the-top tartare with a mix of filet mignon and wagyu beef. The version here uses just prime beef tenderloin.

4 SERVINGS

¼ cup plus 1 teaspoon mayonnaise
2 teaspoons minced flat-leaf parsley
1 teaspoon chopped fresh tarragon
Kosher salt and freshly ground pepper
½ pound best-quality beef tenderloin, cut into ¼-inch dice
2 tablespoons extra-virgin olive oil, plus more for drizzling
2 teaspoons Dijon mustard, plus more for serving
1 teaspoon Worcestershire sauce
1½ tablespoons capers, coarsely chopped
4 tablespoons finely chopped red onion
Crostini, for serving

1. In a bowl, mix ¼ cup of the mayonnaise, 1 teaspoon of the parsley and the tarragon. Season with salt and pepper and refrigerate.

2. In a medium bowl, mix the meat with the 2 tablespoons of olive oil, the remaining 1 teaspoon mayonnaise, the mustard, Worcestershire sauce and capers. Season with salt and pepper. Transfer to a cutting board and finely chop the meat.

3. Transfer the tartare to cold plates. Season with salt and pepper. Sprinkle with the chopped onion and the remaining parsley. Drizzle with olive oil and serve with the herb mayonnaise, mustard and crostini.

Grilled Lamb Bites with Black-Olive Oil

FATHER'S OFFICE •
SANTA MONICA, CA

"This dish epitomizes the style of eating I love," says owner and chef Sang Yoon. "It's informal, easily shared and conducive to drinking and socializing because you just grab a skewer with your fingers." The grilled lamb and its luscious tapenade were inspired by Yoon's travels in southern Spain and North Africa.

8 SERVINGS

½ cup pitted kalamata olives
⅓ cup plus 1 tablespoon extra-virgin olive oil
1 garlic clove, chopped
1 teaspoon finely grated lemon zest
1 teaspoon sherry vinegar
½ teaspoon finely chopped rosemary
2 teaspoons ground cumin
2 teaspoons sweet paprika
1¼ pounds boneless leg of lamb, cut into 1-inch cubes
Salt and freshly ground pepper

1. Light a grill or preheat a grill pan. In a blender, combine the olives with ⅓ cup of the olive oil and puree. Add the garlic, lemon zest, vinegar and rosemary and puree. Transfer to a serving bowl.

2. In a medium bowl, mix the cumin, paprika and the remaining 1 tablespoon of olive oil. Add the lamb and turn to coat. Season with salt and pepper.

3. Grill the lamb over high heat until medium-rare, about 2 minutes per side. Transfer to a plate and let stand for 5 minutes. Skewer each lamb cube with a toothpick. Transfer to a platter and serve with the black-olive oil.

Sloppy Joe Dip

HOME • SAN FRANCISCO
Like all the food at this aptly named San Francisco restaurant (iceberg lettuce with bacon and ranch dressing, Niman Ranch meat loaf with mashed potatoes), this hearty dip is an homage to an all-American classic, served with house-made tortilla chips in place of the usual bun.

6 SERVINGS

1 tablespoon vegetable oil
1 pound ground beef chuck
1 small onion, cut into ¼-inch dice
2 garlic cloves, minced
1 jalapeño, seeded and minced
1½ cups canned chopped tomatoes with their juice
¼ cup ketchup
1½ tablespoons prepared horseradish
1 tablespoon Worcestershire sauce
½ teaspoon celery seeds
Salt and freshly ground pepper
Tortilla chips and sour cream, for serving

In a large skillet, heat the oil. Add the meat, breaking it up with a spoon, and cook over high heat until browned, about 7 minutes. Add the onion and garlic and cook, stirring occasionally, until the onion is translucent, about 3 minutes. Add the jalapeño and cook for 2 minutes. Stir in the tomatoes, ketchup, horseradish, Worcestershire sauce and celery seeds. Cover and cook over low heat for 15 minutes. Season with salt and pepper. Transfer the dip to a bowl and serve hot with tortilla chips and sour cream.

Egg & Harissa Sandwiches

112 EATERY · MINNEAPOLIS
This ingenious take on a bacon and fried egg sandwich, which is brushed with the pungent North African chile paste *harissa*, is chef Isaac Becker's idea of a perfect late-night snack.

4 SERVINGS

- **8** thick bacon slices
- **Eight ½-inch-thick slices best-quality white bread**
- **2** tablespoons extra-virgin olive oil
- **4** large eggs
- **Salt and freshly ground pepper**
- **4** tablespoons *harissa*
- **¼** cup loosely packed cilantro leaves

1. Preheat the oven to 350°. In a large skillet, cook the bacon over moderate heat until crisp, about 6 minutes. Drain on paper towels and cut each piece in half crosswise.

2. Arrange the bread on a baking sheet. Toast in the oven for about 10 minutes, or until lightly golden around the edges.

3. In a large nonstick skillet, heat the olive oil. Fry the eggs over moderate heat until the whites are set and the yolks are still runny, about 2 minutes. Season the eggs with salt and pepper.

4. Spread the *harissa* on the toasted bread. Top 4 pieces of the bread with the bacon, cilantro and fried eggs. Gently break the yolks, close the sandwiches and serve immediately.

Pug Burger

THE HUNGRY CAT · HOLLYWOOD

This delectable blue cheese burger is a best seller at chef David Lentz's restaurant, which is named for, and decorated with pictures of, his two cats, Yoda and Tweetie. "Since my cats have gotten so much press, I thought it was only fair to give my dog Pug some props with this burger," he says.

4 SERVINGS

- 2 pounds lean ground sirloin
- 8 strips applewood-smoked bacon
- ½ cup mayonnaise, plus more for serving
- 1 garlic clove, minced

Kosher salt and freshly ground pepper

- 4 kaiser rolls, split
- 3 tablespoons extra-virgin olive oil
- 3 ounces Danish blue cheese, sliced

Sliced ripe Hass avocado, Bibb lettuce leaves and red onion slices

1. Light a grill. Form the meat into 4 large patties about 1 inch thick. Let stand at room temperature for 30 minutes.

2. In a skillet, cook the bacon over moderate heat until crisp, 6 minutes; drain on paper towels. In a bowl, mix the ½ cup of mayonnaise with the garlic; season with salt and pepper.

3. Brush the cut sides of the rolls with 2 tablespoons of the oil and lightly toast on the grill. Brush the burgers with the remaining oil and season well with salt and pepper. Grill over moderately high heat for 3 minutes; flip and top with the cheese. Cook for 3 more minutes for medium-rare. Spread the bottom roll halves with the garlic mayonnaise. Top with a burger, bacon, avocado, lettuce and onion and serve.

PUG BURGER
The Hungry Cat, Hollywood

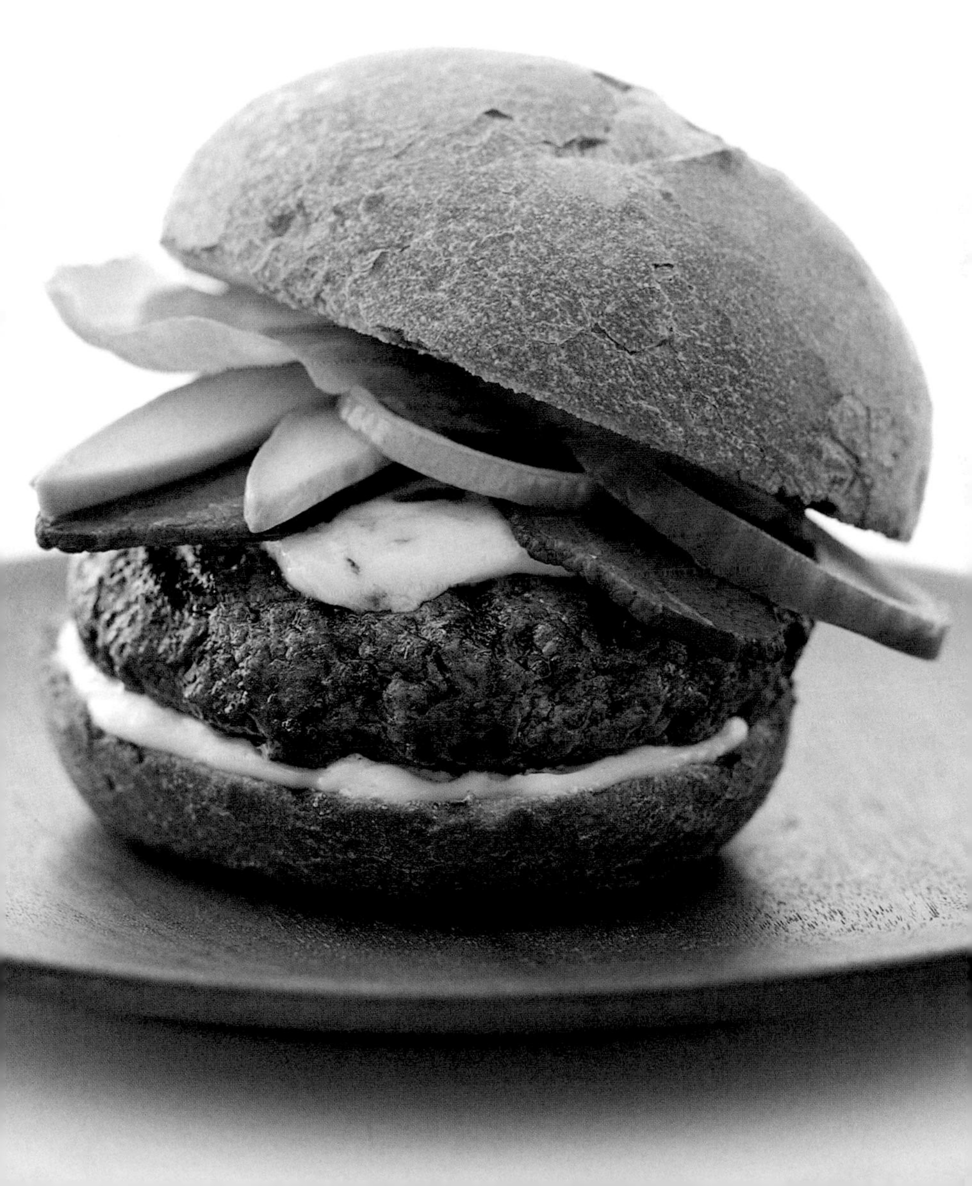

Cubano Sandwiches

THE SPOTTED PIG • NEW YORK CITY

Unlike most *cubano* sandwiches, which are ridiculously greasy, the Spotted Pig's version eschews mayonnaise. Chef April Bloomfield uses ultratender roasted pork shoulder, along with prosciutto, Gruyère and cornichons, to make her delicious sandwich.

4 SERVINGS

¾ cup cornichons, chopped, plus
½ tablespoon cornichon pickling liquid
¼ cup sliced pickled jalapeños, chopped
2 tablespoons drained capers, chopped
3 tablespoons Dijon mustard
4 large French bread rolls, split, or 1 large baguette, cut into 4 pieces
3 tablespoons extra-virgin olive oil
4 cups shredded Gruyère cheese (10 ounces)
2 pounds roasted pork, preferably shoulder, sliced ¼ inch thick
Kosher salt and freshly ground pepper
¼ pound thinly sliced prosciutto

1. Preheat the oven to 375°. In a bowl, mix the cornichons and their pickling liquid with the jalapeños, capers and mustard.

2. Brush the outside of the rolls with the oil and place each on a 12-inch piece of foil, cut side up. Sprinkle ½ cup of Gruyère over the bottom half of each roll. Top with the sliced pork. Spread ¼ cup of the cornichon mixture over the pork and season with salt and pepper. Top with the prosciutto and the remaining Gruyère. Close the sandwiches; tightly roll them up in foil. Bake for 20 minutes, until the cheese is melted and the rolls are crisp. Slice the sandwiches in half on the bias and serve.

Blue Smoke
Black Pepper Ribs

BLUE SMOKE • NEW YORK CITY

Chef Ken Callaghan was inspired to make Blue Smoke's peppery beef ribs after eating his way through Austin. He finalized the recipe in his own smoker in his New Jersey backyard, then put them on the menu at Blue Smoke. You can also use pork ribs, which are more readily available.

8 SERVINGS

- 2 tablespoons coarsely ground pepper
- 2 tablespoons brown sugar
- 1 tablespoon kosher salt
- 1 teaspoon Pimentón de la Vera (smoked Spanish paprika)
- 2 racks pork baby back ribs (about 4½ pounds)

Preheat the oven to 350°. In a small bowl, mix the pepper with the sugar, salt and smoked paprika. Sprinkle both sides of the ribs with the pepper mixture. Place the ribs, meaty side up, on a large rimmed baking sheet. Bake for 2½ hours, or until the meat begins to pull away from the bones. Transfer the ribs to a cutting board and let stand for 5 minutes. Cut the racks into individual ribs and serve.

Best Nightlife
2007

Best Nightlife

Here's a listing of the restaurants, bars and lounges that created the incredible cocktails in this book (see page numbers below for the recipes), plus other hot spots you should know about.

ASPEN

39 Degrees
P. 140
Mountainside hangout
Sky Hotel
709 E. Durant Ave.
970-429-7860

The Century Room
Stately dining room
Hotel Jerome
330 E. Main St.
970-920-1000

Double Dog Pub
Subterranean watering hole
305 E. Hopkins Ave.
970-925-3459

Montagna
Resort hotel restaurant
The Little Nell
675 E. Durant Ave.
970-920-4600

Pacifica Seafood & Raw Bar
Hip brasserie
307 S. Mill St.
970-920-9775

ATLANTA AREA

Aiko
Trendy sushi bar and martini lounge
128 E. Andrews Dr.
404-869-4800

Bacchanalia
P. 23
Urbane dining room in a renovated factory
1198 Howell Mill Rd.
404-365-0410

Bluepointe
Asian-inflected New American
3455 Peachtree Rd.
404-237-9070

Dolce Enoteca e Ristorante
Slick sibling of a West Hollywood hot spot
Atlantic Station
261 19th St.
404-872-3902

Ecco
Wood-fired pizza specialist
40 Seventh St.
404-347-9555

Emeril's Atlanta
P. 53
Star chef's outpost
3500 Lenox Rd.
404-564-5600

Lotus Lounge
Upscale nightclub
Lindbergh City Center
2420 Piedmont Rd. NE
404-869-3445

Milton's Cuisine & Cocktails
Restaurant and bar in a restored farmhouse
780 Mayfield Rd., Alpharetta
770-817-0161

No Mas Cantina
Tequila temple
180 Walker St.
404-574-5678

Restaurant Eugene
P. 82
Discreetly opulent dining room
2277 Peachtree Rd.
404-355-0321

The Standard
Fun neighborhood watering hole
327 Memorial Dr.
404-681-3344

Trois
P. 121
Sleek three-story brasserie and bar
1180 Peachtree St.
404-815-3337

ATLANTIC CITY

Bobby Flay Steak
P. 68
Grill master's chic chophouse
Borgata Hotel Casino & Spa
1 Borgata Way
866-692-6742

SeaBlue
Star chef's East Coast outpost
Borgata Hotel Casino & Spa
1 Borgata Way
866-692-6742

Wolfgang Puck American Grille
Casual tavern and upscale dining room
Borgata Hotel Casino & Spa
1 Borgata Way
866-692-6742

AUSTIN

The Belmont
Rat Pack era–inspired restaurant and lounge
305 W. Sixth St.
512-457-0300

Bess Bistro on Pecan
Homey dining room in a 1918 building
500 W. Sixth St.
512-477-2377

Jeffrey's Restaurant & Bar
P. 46
Inventive New American
1204 W. Lynn St.
512-477-5584

Ranch 616
South Texas tavern
616 Nueces St.
512-479-7616

Sabores Seafood & Clam Bar
Shellfish mecca
7517 Cameron Rd.
512-371-3877

BOSTON AREA

28 Degrees
P. 176
Chic martini bar
1 Appleton St.
617-728-0728

Blu
Luxe health club's restaurant
The Sports Club/LA
4 Avery St.
617-375-8550

Dbar
Irish pub turned hip nightspot
1236 Dorchester Ave.
Dorchester
617-265-4490

Eastern Standard
P. 23
Relaxed hotel restaurant
528 Commonwealth Ave.
617-532-9100

Gargoyles on the Square
Davis Square bistro and bar
219 Elm St., Somerville
617-776-5300

No. 9 Park
P. 80
French-Italian foodie favorite
9 Park St.
617-742-9991

Radius
P. 43
Star chef's flagship
8 High St.
617-426-1234

Revolution Rock Bar
Music lover's dream spot
200 High St.
617-261-4200

RhumBar
Rum-centric Harvard Square lounge
Om Restaurant/Lounge
92 Winthrop St., Cambridge
617-576-2800

Sibling Rivalry
P. 71
Chef brothers serve competing menus
525 Tremont St.
617-338-5338

Toro
P. 110
Lively South End tapas bar
1704 Washington St.
617-536-4300

Cordavi
Haute food haven
14 N. Market St.
843-577-0090

High Cotton
P. 48
*Renovated 18th-century
warehouse*
199 E. Bay St.
843-724-3815

McCrady's
*Modern restaurant in
a historic building*
2 Unity Alley
843-577-0025

Mercato
City Market trattoria
102 N. Market St.
843-722-6393

Thoroughbred Club
P. 111
Genteel cocktail lounge
Charleston Place hotel
205 Meeting St.
843-722-4900

Tristan
*Bold, modern, global spot
with a Dublin-born chef*
55 S. Market St.
843-534-2155

BB's
P. 171
New gastropub
22 E. Hubbard St.
312-755-0007

Clark Street Ale House
P. 72
*Retro tavern and
cigar bar*
742 N. Clark St.
312-642-9253

Custom House
P. 43
Artisanal steak house
500 S. Dearborn St.
312-523-0200

David Burke's Primehouse
P. 84
Innovative steak house
The James Chicago hotel
616 N. Rush St.
312-660-6000

Del Toro Café y Taberna
P. 152
Modern tapas bar
1520 N. Damen Ave.
773-252-1500

Las Palmas
P. 100
Margarita destination
1835 W. North Ave.
773-289-4991

The Matchbox
Pint-size barroom
770 N. Milwaukee Ave.
312-666-9292

The Motel Bar
P. 120
Swank 1970s-style lounge
600 W. Chicago Ave.
312-822-2900

Moxie
P. 132
Lively tapas and martini joint
3517 N. Clark St.
773-935-6694

Nacional 27
P. 170
*Pan-Latin restaurant
and salsa club*
325 W. Huron St.
312-664-2727

North Pond
*Seasonal restaurant in an
Arts & Crafts–style space*
2610 N. Cannon Dr.
773-477-5845

Parlor
P. 160
Mod diner classics
1745 W. North Ave.
773-782-9000

Pump Room
Local institution since 1938
1301 N. State Pkwy.
312-266-0360

Sidebar Grille
*After-work haunt with
a law-office look*
221 N. LaSalle St.
312-739-3900

Stone Lotus
Spa-focused lounge
873 N. Orleans St.
312-440-9680

Tryst
Small plates and martini boîte
3485 N. Clark St.
773-755-3980

Vie
Suburban gem
4471 Lawn Ave.
Western Springs
708-246-2082

DALLAS/FORT WORTH AREA

Abacus
Contemporary global menu
4511 McKinney Ave., Dallas
214-559-3111

Jasper's
Suave grill house
7161 Bishop Rd., Plano
469-229-9111

**The Lonesome Dove
Western Bistro**
Sophisticated cowboy cuisine
2406 N. Main St., Fort Worth
817-740-8810

Luqa & Petrus Lounge
*New American above an
art gallery*
1217 Main St., Dallas
214-760-9000

Shinsei
Pan-Asian hot spot
7713 Inwood Rd., Dallas
214-352-0005

Sonoma Grill & Wine Bar
West Coast–inspired bistro
380 Parker Sq., Flower Mound
972-899-8989

Stephan Pyles
*Star chef's nouveau
Southwestern restaurant*
1807 Ross Ave.
Dallas
214-580-7000

Trece
P. 98
Tequila stronghold
4513 Travis St., Dallas
214-780-1900

Vue & Nine7Two
*Sprawling dining room
and lounge*
5100 Beltline Road, Dallas
972-788-1928

Bistro Vendôme
P. 138
Parisian-style bistro
1420 Larimer St., Denver
303-825-3232

Corner Bar
Aristocratic tavern
Hotel Boulderado
2115 13th St., Boulder
303-442-4560

Duo
*Homey sustainability-minded
restaurant*
2413 W. 32nd Ave., Denver
303-477-4141

Frasca Food & Wine
P. 149
Italian canteen
1738 Pearl St., Boulder
303-442-6966

Nine75
*Martini and comfort food
hangout*
975 Lincoln St., Denver
303-975-0975

Summit
P. 57
*Adam Tihany–designed
restaurant in the Rockies*
The Broadmoor
19 Lake Cir., Colorado Springs
719-577-5896

Trilogy Wine Bar & Lounge
Hip local favorite with live music
2017 13th St., Boulder
303-473-9463

West End Tavern
Bar for bourbon barons
926 Pearl St., Boulder
303-444-3535

HONOLULU

Bar 35
Lively Chinatown bar
35 N. Hotel St.
808-537-3535

La Mariana Sailing Club
Old-school tiki bar
50 Sand Island Access Rd.
808-848-2800

Lewers Lounge
P. 62
Mixologist mecca
Halekulani
2199 Kalia Rd.
808-923-2311

Next Door
Live music and indie-film lounge
43 N. Hotel St.
808-548-6398

Thirtyninehotel
Art gallery and dance club
39 N. Hotel St.
808-599-2552

HOUSTON

Arturo's Uptown Italiano
*Regional Italian
restaurant and bar*
1180-1 Uptown Park Blvd.
713-621-1180

Backstreet Café
*Garden dining behind
a 1930s house*
1103 S. Shepherd Dr.
713-521-2239

Glass Wall
Houston Heights bistro
933 Studewood St.
713-868-7930

Hugo's
P. 61
Tequila and mezcal destination
1600 Westheimer Rd.
713-524-7744

Indika
Modern Indian
516 Westheimer Rd.
713-524-2170

KANSAS CITY, MO

12 Baltimore
Swank tavern
Hotel Phillips
106 W. 12th St.
816-346-4410

Bluestem
New American foodie favorite
900 Westport Rd.
816-561-1101

JP Wine Bar
P. 32
Crossroads Arts District oasis
1526 Walnut St.
816-842-2660

Velvet Dog
Martini mecca
400 E. 31st St.
816-753-9990

LAS VEGAS

Bellagio Pool Bar
P. 30
Gardenside getaway
Bellagio hotel & casino
3600 S. Las Vegas Blvd.
702-693-7111

Boa Steakhouse
P. 118
Posh meat lover's spot
Caesars, The Forum Shops
3500 S. Las Vegas Blvd.
702-733-7373

Cabo Mexican Restaurant
Colorful desert cantina
Red Rock Casino Resort & Spa
11011 W. Charleston Blvd.
702-797-7576

Club Privé
P. 54
High-stakes casino lounge
Bellagio hotel & casino
3600 S. Las Vegas Blvd.
702-693-7111

Commander's Palace
P. 27
New Orleans outpost
Desert Passage at Aladdin
3663 S. Las Vegas Blvd.
702-892-8272

Lure
Indigo-hued ultralounge
Wynn Las Vegas
3131 S. Las Vegas Blvd.
702-770-3633

Nora's Cuisine
P. 165
Sicilian experts
6020 W. Flamingo Rd., #10
702-873-8990

Restaurant Guy Savoy
French star's outpost
Caesars Palace
3570 S. Las Vegas Blvd.
877-346-4642

Rosemary's Restaurant
*New American with
a Southern accent*
8125 W. Sahara Ave.
702-869-2251

Social House
Sushi sanctuary
Treasure Island
3300 S. Las Vegas Blvd.
702-894-7223

Stack
New American bistro
The Mirage hotel
3400 S. Las Vegas Blvd.
702-792-7800

27 Lobster & Surf Shack
(seasonal)
Cajun-accented seafood
2095 Montauk Hwy.
Amagansett
631-267-6980

Annona
*Italian restaurant above
a luxury car showroom*
112 Riverhead Rd.
Westhampton Beach
631-288-7766

Besito
Tequila hotbed
402 New York Ave.
Huntington
631-549-0100

Jedediah Hawkins Inn
Renovated mansion
400 S. Jamesport Ave.
Jamesport
631-722-2900

Nick & Toni's
Celebrity mainstay
136 N. Main St.
East Hampton
631-324-3550

The Patio
Gardenside dining room
54 Main St.
Westhampton Beach
631-288-4878

Red/bar Brasserie
Fashionista favorite
210 Hampton Rd.
Southampton
631-283-0704

Bin 8945 Wine Bar & Bistro
PP. 92, 177
*Small-plates wine bar
with great cocktails*
8945 Santa Monica Blvd.
West Hollywood
310-550-8945

Bridge
Posh Italian canteen
755 N. La Cienega Blvd.
Los Angeles
310-659-3535

Cut
P. 180
*Wolfgang Puck's trendy
steak house*
The Beverly Wilshire hotel
9500 Wilshire Blvd.
Beverly Hills
310-276-8500

East/West Lounge
West Hollywood hideaway
8851 Santa Monica Blvd.
West Hollywood
310-360-6186

Eleven
P. 158
Sprawling supper club
8811 Santa Monica Blvd.
West Hollywood
310-855-0800

Father's Office
P. 181
European-style tavern
1018 Montana Ave.
Santa Monica
310-393-2337

Hatfield's
P. 146
*Husband and wife's
California-French spot*
7458 Beverly Blvd.
Los Angeles
323-935-2977

The Hungry Cat
PP. 81, 184
Fancy clam and burger shack
1535 N. Vine St., Hollywood
323-462-2155

Hyde Lounge
P. 71
A-listers' haunt
8029 W. Sunset Blvd.
West Hollywood
323-656-4933

J Restaurant & Lounge
Cavernous megalounge
1119 S. Olive St., Los Angeles
213-746-7746

Katsuya
P. 35
*Philippe Starck–
designed sushi boîte*
11777 San Vicente Blvd.
Los Angeles
310-207-8744

Lucques
P. 123
California-French standout
8474 Melrose Ave.
Los Angeles
323-655-6277

Providence
PP. 52, 133
Seafood Shangri-la
5955 Melrose Ave.
Los Angeles
323-460-4170

Social Hollywood
P. 104
VIP playground
6525 W. Sunset Blvd.
Los Angeles
323-462-5222

Sona
P. 42
New-fashioned French
401 N. La Cienega Blvd.
Los Angeles
310-659-7708

Stonehill Tavern
P. 160
Elegant dining room
with an ocean view
St. Regis Resort Monarch Beach
1 Monarch Beach Resort
Dana Point
949-234-3318

LOUISVILLE

Avalon
New American bistro
1314 Bardstown Rd.
502-454-5336

Bourbons Bistro
Southern-inspired dining
and 100-plus bourbons
2255 Frankfort Ave.
502-894-8838

Jack Fry's Restaurant
Bistro and live jazz in
a former saloon
1007 Bardstown Rd.
502-452-9244

Maker's Mark Bourbon
House & Lounge
Bourbon experts
Fourth Street Live
446 S. Fourth St.
502-568-9009

Park Place on Main
P. 98
Cocktail craftsmen
at a piano bar
401 E. Main St.
502-515-0172

Proof on Main
P. 153
Art-filled restaurant with
a great bourbon selection
21c Museum Hotel
702 W. Main St.
502-217-6360

Seviche
P. 74
Seafood-centric Nuevo Latino
1538 Bardstown Rd.
502-473-8560

MADISON, WI

Cocoliquot
P. 65
French bistro and chocolate
haven
225 King St.
608-255-2626

Maduro
P. 96
Cigar and whiskey
connoisseurs' hangout
117 E. Main St.
608-294-9371

Natt Spil
P. 67
Norwegian-inspired speakeasy
211 King St.
608-258-8787

Osteria Papavero
P. 30
Rustic trattoria
128 E. Wilson St.
608-255-8376

Restaurant Magnus
P. 48
*Latin-flavored champion
of local farmers*
120 E. Wilson St.
608-258-8787

Smoky's Club
P. 78
1950s-era steak house
3005 University Ave.
608-233-2120

Tornado Steak House
P. 138
Downtown chophouse
116 S. Hamilton St.
608-256-3570

MIAMI/FORT LAUDERDALE AREA

Below Zero Nitro-Bar
Avant-garde cocktail lounge
Barton G.
1427 West Ave., Miami Beach
305-672-8881

ElboRoom
Beachfront hangout since 1938
241 S. Fort Lauderdale
Beach Blvd.
Fort Lauderdale
954-463-4615

Ginger Grove
P. 38
Asian-inspired dining room
Mayfair Hotel and Spa
3000 Florida Ave.
Coconut Grove
305-779-5100

Jackson's Steakhouse
*Mens' club–like drinking
and dining quarters*
450 E. Las Olas Blvd.
Fort Lauderdale
954-522-4450

Karu & Y
Overtown hot spot
71 NW 14th St., Miami
305-403-7850

La Goulue Christian Delouvrier
*Palm tree–lined
indoor-outdoor bistro*
9700 Collins Ave.
Bal Harbour
305-865-2181

Mokaï
See-and-be-seen scene
235 23rd St.
Miami Beach
305-531-4166

Rose Bar
People-watching paradise
Delano hotel
1685 Collins Ave., Miami Beach
305-672-2000

Shirttail Charlie's
Dockside seafood joint
400 SW 3rd Ave.
Fort Lauderdale
954-463-3474

Toscano Grille
*Pasta and wood-fired
fish specialists*
2120 Salzedo St., Coral Gables
305-448-5111

Trina Restaurant & Lounge
P. 35
Drinks destination
The Atlantic hotel
601 N. Fort Lauderdale
Beach Blvd.
Fort Lauderdale
954-567-8070

Wish
*Todd Oldham–designed
indoor-outdoor restaurant*
The Hotel
801 Collins Ave., Miami Beach
305-674-9474

MINNEAPOLIS

112 Eatery
P. 183
Local chefs' favorite
112 N. 3rd St.
612-343-7696

Cosmos
Mod hotel restaurant
Graves 601 Hotel
601 First Ave. North
612-312-1168

La Belle Vie
*Posh French restaurant
and lounge*
510 Groveland Ave.
612-874-6440

Masa
P. 102
Elegant regional Mexican
1070 Nicollet Mall
612-338-6272

Spoonriver
Stylish greenmarket dining
750 S. Second St.
612-436-2236

Town Talk Diner
P. 116
*Upscale comfort food in
a renovated 1940s diner*
2707½ E. Lake St.
612-722-1312

NAPA VALLEY/SONOMA COUNTY

Barndiva
P. 50
Salute to sustainable farming
231 Center St., Healdsburg
707-431-0100

Cyrus
P. 143
Regal wine-country restaurant
29 North St., Healdsburg
707-433-3311

Redd
Winemakers' hangout
6480 Washington St.
Yountville
707-944-2222

Cabana
Southern bistro and bar
1910 Belcourt Ave.
615-577-2262

Mirror
Miami-style small-plates boîte
2317 12th Ave. South
615-383-8330

Sambuca
Funky supper club and live music venue
601 12th Ave. South
615-248-2888

Virago
Asian-inspired restaurant and sushi bar
1811 Division St.
615-320-5149

Watermark Restaurant
Elegant space with skyline views
507 12th Ave. South
615-254-2000

Antoine's Restaurant
French Quarter landmark
713 St. Louis St.
504-581-4422

Arnaud's French 75 Bar
P. 136
Dapper, cigar-friendly spot
813 Bienville St.
866-230-8895

Carousel Lounge
P. 136
Festive revolving bar
Hotel Monteleone
214 Royale St.
504-523-3341

Dick & Jenny's
Local favorite with a courtyard and porch swings
4501 Tchoupitoulas St.
504-894-9880

Galatoire's
Elevated Creole
209 Bourbon St.
504-525-2021

Herbsaint
P. 32
Neo-Creole standout
701 St. Charles Ave.
504-524-4114

Lilette
Airy French-Italian bistro
3637 Magazine St.
504-895-1636

Old Absinthe House
P. 139
Bourbon Street pioneer
240 Bourbon St.
504-523-3181

5 Ninth
PP. 114, 129
*Modern restaurant in
an 1840s brownstone*
5 Ninth Ave., Manhattan
212-929-9460

Aspen
P. 119
Urban après-ski
30 W. 22nd St., Manhattan
212-645-5040

Barmarché
P. 20
Intimate neighborhood bistro
14 Spring St., Manhattan
212-219-2399

Blue Smoke
P. 187
*Barbecue joint with
jazz downstairs*
116 E. 27th St., Manhattan
212-447-7733

Brandy Library
PP. 65, 90
Cocktail scholars
25 N. Moore St., Manhattan
212-226-5545

Brooklyn Social
*Hip bar in a former Sicilian
men's club*
335 Smith St., Brooklyn
718-858-7758

Buddakan
P. 54
Asian mega-restaurant
75 Ninth Ave., Manhattan
212-989-6699

Cookshop
P. 42
*Innovative American
comfort food*
156 10th Ave., Manhattan
212-924-4440

Country
P. 34
*New American in a
Beaux Arts hotel*
The Carlton hotel
90 Madison Ave., Manhattan
212-889-7100

Del Posto
PP. 26, 164
Mario Batali showpiece
85 10th Ave., Manhattan
212-497-8090

Devin Tavern
P. 86
Upscale old-world tavern
363 Greenwich St., Manhattan
212-334-7337

Dressler
*Elegant wrought iron–accented
dining room*
149 Broadway, Brooklyn
718-384-6343

Employees Only
P. 122
Bartender-owned supper club
510 Hudson St., Manhattan
212-242-3021

Flatiron Lounge
PP. 93, 159
Mixologists' headquarters
37 W. 19th St., Manhattan
212-727-7741

Franny's
P. 36
Top-shelf pizza spot
295 Flatbush Ave., Brooklyn
718-230-0221

Freemans
PP. 115, 174
Back-alley hideaway
Freeman Alley, Manhattan
212-420-0012

The Good Fork
P. 178
Red Hook nook
391 Van Brunt St., Brooklyn
718-643-6636

Gramercy Tavern
PP. 85, 96
New American stalwart
42 E. 20th St., Manhattan
212-477-0777

Jack the Horse Tavern
P. 119
Quaint corner restaurant
66 Hicks St., Brooklyn
718-852-5084

Little Branch
P. 60
*Subterranean bar for
drink classicists*
20-22 Seventh Ave. South
Manhattan
212-929-4360

The Little Owl
P. 22
Stellar West Village bistro
90 Bedford St., Manhattan
212-741-4695

The Modern
P. 68
Sleek museum restaurant
9 W. 53rd St., Manhattan
212-333-1220

Pegu Club
PP. 100, 122
Cocktail connoisseurs' haunt
77 W. Houston St., 2nd Fl.
Manhattan
212-473-7348

Perry St.
P. 56
*Star chef Vongerichten's
Hudson River outpost*
176 Perry St., Manhattan
212-352-1900

P*ONG
P. 27
Small-plates boîte
150 W. 10th St., Manhattan
212-929-0898

The Red Cat
P. 50
*Polished restaurant and bar
with a New England vibe*
227 10th Ave., Manhattan
212-242-1122

Room 4 Dessert
P. 31
Cocktail and dessert alchemists
17 Cleveland Pl., Manhattan
212-941-5405

The Spotted Pig
PP. 150, 186
West Village gastropub
314 W. 11th St., Manhattan
212-620-0393

The Stanton Social
P. 165
*1940s-inspired Lower East
Side lounge*
99 Stanton St., Manhattan
212-995-0099

Tabla
P. 158
Creative Indian-American
11 Madison Ave., Manhattan
212-889-0667

Tailor
P. 142
Soho dessert and cocktail hub
525 Broome St., Manhattan
tailornyc.com

The Tasting Room
P. 22
Seasonal drink specialists
264 Elizabeth St., Manhattan
212-358-7831

Trestle on Tenth
P. 92
Swiss-accented New American
242 10th Ave., Manhattan
212-645-5659

WD-50
P. 67
Futuristic food mecca
50 Clinton St., Manhattan
212-477-2900

NORTHERN & CENTRAL
NEW JERSEY

Bar Majestic
*1920s burlesque theater
turned tapas bar*
275 Grove St., Jersey City
201-451-4400

Catherine Lombardi
P. 24
Flamboyant Italian-American
3 Livingston Ave.
New Brunswick
732-296-9463

Pluckemin Inn
P. 130
*New American in
a restored former inn*
359 Rte. 202/206 South
Bedminster
908-658-9292

Stage Left
Elegant New American
5 Livingston Ave.
New Brunswick
732-828-4444

PHILADELPHIA

Alfa Restaurant & Bar
Shared-plates meeting place
1709 Walnut St.
215-751- 0201

Alma de Cuba
*Sleek red, white and black
dining room and lounge*
1623 Walnut St.
215-988-1799

Amada
PP. 80, 175
*Tapas and Pedro Almodóvar–
inspired cocktails*
217-219 Chestnut St.
215-625-2450

Bamboo Lounge
Shadowy second-floor cloister
101 N. 20th St.
215-636-0228

The Continental Mid-Town
Space-age retro lounge
1801 Chestnut St.
215-567-1800

Cuba Libre
P. 133
Old Havana–inspired rum spot
10 S. Second St.
215-627-0666

London Grill
P. 62
Art-museum-district pub
2301 Fairmount Ave.
215-978-4545

Morimoto
P. 53
Iron Chef's domain
723 Chestnut St.
215-413-9070

Pod
Mod Asian-fusion
3636 Sansom St.
215-387-1803

Tangerine
Casbah-inspired Mediterranean
232 Market St.
215-627-5116

**Water Works Restaurant
& Lounge**
*Grand dining room
on the Schyulkill River*
640 Water Works Dr.
215-236-9000

Baroque Luxe Lounge
London-inspired destination
20751 N. Pima Rd., Scottsdale
480-563-5893

Méthode Bistro
Candlelit Mediterranean
6204 N. Scottsdale Rd.
Scottsdale
480-998-8220

Olive & Ivy
Cal-Med restaurant and market
7135 E. Camelback Rd.
Scottsdale
480-751-2200

Ticoz Resto-Bar
Laid-back Latin
5114 N. Seventh St., Phoenix
602-200-0160

Tradiciones
Mariachi and margarita mecca
1602 E. Roosevelt St., Phoenix
602-254-1719

PORTLAND, OR

23Hoyt
Intimate New American
529 NW 23rd Ave.
503-445-7400

Andina
P. 75
Nuevo-Peruvian gem
1314 NW Glisan St.
503-228-9535

Café Castagna
P. 26
Comfort-food bistro
1758 SE Hawthorne Blvd.
503-231-9959

Graze
*Pearl District tapas
and cocktail rendezvous*
939 NW 10th Ave.
503-808-9888

Mint/820
P. 39
Chic inky-black lounge
816 N. Russell St.
503-284-5518

Park Kitchen
PP. 148, 172
*Food lover's haunt
in a historic building*
422 NW Eighth St.
503-223-7275

Roux
P. 139
Creole hot spot
1700 N. Killingsworth St.
503-285-1200

Saucebox
P. 78
Creative pan-Asian
214 SW Broadway
503-241-3393

An
Bold French-Vietnamese
2800 Renaissance Park Pl., Cary
919-677-9229

Bin 54
P. 126
Chic steak house
1201-M Raleigh Rd., Chapel Hill
919-969-1155

Federal
Hip tavern
914 W. Main St., Durham
919-680-8611

Jujube
Pan-Asian haven
1201-L Raleigh Rd., Chapel Hill
919-960-0555

Lantern
P. 86
*Romantic, lantern-lit
restaurant and bar*
423 W. Franklin St., Chapel Hill
919-969-8846

Vivace
Stylish trattoria
4209 Lassiter Mill Rd., #115
Raleigh
919-787-7747

Baleen San Diego
P. 128
Bayfront dining room
Paradise Point Resort & Spa
1404 Vacation Rd., San Diego
858-490-6363

Cendio
Modern Latin American
909 Prospect St., La Jolla
858-454-9664

Jack's La Jolla
P. 129
*Sprawling drinking and dining
destination with a piano bar*
7863 Girard Ave., La Jolla
858-456-8111

Modus
*Urbane Banker's Hill
meeting place*
2202 Fourth Ave., San Diego
619-236-8516

Absinthe Brasserie & Bar
PP. 107, 115
Belle Epoque–style brasserie
398 Hayes St.
415-551-1590

The Alembic
P. 88
Newfangled pub
1725 Haight St.
415-666-0822

Bix
Swank supper club
56 Gold St.
415-433-6300

Bong Su
P. 70
Trendy Vietnamese
311 Third St.
415-536-5800

Bourbon & Branch
P. 110
*1920s-inspired reservations-
only speakeasy*
501 Jones St.
bourbonandbranch.com

Cortez
P. 85
*Buzzing boutique-hotel
restaurant and bar*
Hotel Adagio
550 Geary St.
415-292-6360

Farmer Brown
P. 159
Neo-Southern soul food
25 Mason St.
415-409-3276

First Crush
*Relaxed Union Square
bistro and wine bar*
101 Cyril Magnin St.
415-982-7874

Harry Denton's Starlight Room
P. 140
Legendary hotel bar
Sir Francis Drake Hotel
450 Powell St.
415-395-8595

Home
P. 182
Comfort food hangout
2032 Union St.
415-931-5006

MarketBar
*Seasonal Mediterranean
with al fresco dining*
1 Ferry Building, #36
415-434-1100

Martini Monkey
P. 89
Tiki-themed airport bar
Minetta San Jose National
Airport
1661 Airport Dr., Terminal C
San Jose
408-925-9376

Michael Mina
P. 123
Star chef's New American
Westin St. Francis hotel
335 Powell St.
415-397-9222

Nopa
P. 60
Neighborhood gem
560 Divisadero St.
415-864-8643

Range
P. 49
Buzzing Mission District restaurant
842 Valencia St.
415-282-8283

Rye
P. 132
Smooth new bar with vintage pool tables
688 Geary St.
415-786-7803

The Slanted Door
P. 155
Star chef's modern Vietnamese
1 Ferry Building, #3
415-861-8032

Solstice Restaurant & Lounge
P. 154
Small-plates mecca
2801 California St.
415-359-1222

Tres Agaves
P. 107
Tequila kingpin
130 Townsend St.
415-227-0500

Two
P. 103
Laid-back New American
22 Hawthorne St.
415-777-9779

SEATTLE AREA

BOKA Kitchen & Bar
PP. 154, 162
Trendy boutique-hotel creation
1010 First Ave.
206-357-9000

Canlis
P. 84
Frank Lloyd Wright–inspired restaurant and piano lounge
2576 Aurora Ave. North
206-283-3313

Hazlewood
P. 114
Tiny drink den
2311 NW Market St.
206-783-0478

Licorous
P. 52
Mod lounge
928 12th Ave.
206-325-6947

Marjorie
P. 64
Colorful Belltown bistro with a great garden
2331 Second Ave.
206-441-9842

Palisade
Dockside dining spot
2601 W. Marina Pl.
206-285-1000

Sambar
P. 44
French-accented mini-lounge
425 NW Market St.
206-781-4883

Vessel
P. 74
Haute cocktail haunt
1312 Fifth Ave.
206-652-5222

Waterstreet Café & Bar
P. 106
*New American restaurant
in a historic building*
610 Water St. SW, Olympia
360-709-9090

Zig Zag Cafe
P. 66
Refuge near Pike Place Market
501 Western Ave., #202
206-625-1146

WASHINGTON, DC AREA

Agraria
P. 47
*Sophisticated farmer-owned
restaurant*
3000 K St. NW
202-298-0003

Bar Rouge
Urban hideaway
Rouge Hotel
1315 16th St. NW
202-232-8000

Black's Bar & Kitchen
*Modern oyster bar and
fish house*
7750 Woodmont Ave.
Bethesda, MD
301-652-5525

Blue Duck Tavern
P. 126
*Dashing restaurant with
a wood-burning oven*
Park Hyatt Washington hotel
1201 24th St. NW
202-419-6755

Indigo Landing
P. 112
*Low-country restaurant
on the Potomac*
1 Marina Dr., Alexandria, VA
703-548-0001

Mandu
Authentic Korean
1805 18th St. NW
202-588-1540

PS 7's
P. 168
*Penn Quarter small-plates
destination*
777 I St. NW
202-742-8550

PX
P. 99
Glamorous speakeasy
728 King St., Alexandria, VA
703-299-8384

The Red & The Black
New Orleans–inspired tavern
1212 H St. NE
202-399-3201

Urbana
P. 31
*Sleek subterranean
restaurant and wine bar*
2121 P St. NW
202-956-6650

Zola
P. 37
*Spy-themed American
restaurant*
800 F St. NW
202-654-0999

Resource Guide

Here's a list of the best bar must-haves and where you can find them.

GARNISHES

Les Parisiennes Cherries in Brandy
These fresh cherries soaked in kirsch are even better than homemade ones that take a month to make.
SOURCE: emarkys.com

Luxardo Cherries
For this top-of-the-line brand, the cherries are macerated in maraschino liqueur, a clear spirit made from marasca cherries (ironically, there's no maraschino liqueur in the bright-red, artificially colored and flavored maraschino cherries).
SOURCE: hitimewine.net

BITTERS

Fee Brothers Mint, Peach, Orange, Lemon and Aromatic Bitters
For 144 years, this Rochester, New York–based company has been producing bitters in both popular and esoteric flavors with straightforward fruit and herbal accents.
SOURCE: kalustyans.com and surfasonline.com

Peychaud's Bitters
Originally made in New Orleans and based on an 18th-century recipe, these bitters have bright anise and cranberry flavors.
SOURCE: buffalotrace.com

Regans' Orange Bitters
Cocktail guru Gary Regan created these spicy orange peel–infused bitters in his home kitchen before selling them commercially.
SOURCE: buffalotrace.com

SYRUPS

D'Arbo Elderflower and Raspberry Syrups
These wonderfully fruity mixers are made in Austria by a company that dates back to 1879.
SOURCE: farawayfoods.com

Depaz Cane Syrup
This unrefined sugar syrup from Martinique has rich cane flavor; it can be used in place of simple syrup for drinks made with rum.
SOURCE: igourmet.com

Kassatly Chtaura Almond Syrup

This Middle Eastern almond syrup has a wonderful flowery scent.

SOURCE: sos-chefs.com

Monin Almond Syrup

Unlike most almond syrups sold at coffee shops, the French Monin brand is bright, nutty and not too sweet.

SOURCE: moninstore.com

Mymoune Rose Syrup

Unlike most artificially flavored rose syrups, this pink-hued Lebanese syrup, also called *shareb el ward,* is actually made from rose petals.

SOURCE: buylebanese.com

HERBS & SPICES

Cinchona Bark or Quinine

The bark of cinchona trees produces quinine and it gives homemade tonic water an alluring bitterness.

SOURCE: rain-tree.com

Citric Acid or Lemon Salt

A key ingredient in homemade grenadine, citric acid is a nonalcoholic preservative derived from citrus fruit that also adds tang.

SOURCE: bestturkishfood.com

BAR EQUIPMENT

Mr. Mojito Muddlers

Muddlers are used to crush ingredients together to mix and release flavors. Look for large ones that are comfortable to hold and avoid models that are painted or shellacked; veneers can chip into the drink. Mister Mojito makes a good plastic muddler.

SOURCE: mistermojito.com

Tovolo Ice Cube Trays

The best shaken drinks are made with large ice cubes, which melt more slowly than smaller ones. Use ice trays like the silicone ones by Tovolo, which make at least 1-by-1-inch cubes. Silicone trays are better than the reinforced plastic kind because the cubes are easier to pop out.

SOURCE: surlatable.com

GENERAL BAR SUPPLIES

Barstore.com is a terrific one-stop shopping site, selling everything from channel knives for making citrus twists to jiggers in a range of sizes. And its products are competitively priced.

SOURCE: webtender.barstore.com

Glassware Guide

GIN

P. 79: "Atalante" martini glass by Christofle, 212-308-9390 or christofle.com; "Binary" light (background) by Jeremy Pyles from Niche Modern, 212-777-2101 or nichemodern.com.

P. 83: "Mikumi" tumbler by Eastern Accent, 978-443-4308; "Orion" bowl (background) by Nouvel Studio, nouvelstudio.com.

P. 87: "Volcano" tumbler by Arik Levy from Gaia & Gino, gaiaandgino.com.

TEQUILA

P. 94: "Norwood" crystal martini glass by Ralph Lauren Home, 888-475-7674 or rlhome.polo.com; vase from the End of History, 212-647-7598.

P. 97: "Anoushka" tumbler by William Yeoward Crystal, 212-532-2358 or williamyeowardcrystal.com.

P. 101: "Mikumi" stem glass by Eastern Accent, 978-443-4308.

P. 105: "Presage" double old-fashioned glass by Waterford, 800-955-1550 or waterford.com.

WHISKEY

P. 108: "Stem" martini glass by Eastern Accent, 978-443-4308; "H2O" classic bar glass by Riedel, 732-346-8960 or riedel.com; hors d'oeuvre pick and "Uma" decanter from Crate & Barrel, 800-967-6696 or crateandbarrel.com.

P. 113: "Cluny" highball glass by Christofle, 212-308-9390 or christofle.com.

P. 117: "Graham" footed water goblet by Juliska, juliska.com.

BRANDY

P. 127: "O" martini glass by Riedel, 732-346-8960 or riedel.com.

P. 131: "Alto" cocktail glass by Calvin Klein, 877-256-7373.

Acknowledgments

Thank you This collection of recipes would not have been possible without the help of these people.

Tony Abou-Ganim
Erik Adkins
Colin Alevras
Scott Beattie
Jacques Bezuidenhout
Sean Bigley
Jared Brown
Katy Casbarian
Scott Clime
Terry Coughlin
Dale DeGroff
Martin Doudoroff
Ben Dougherty
Christine Ehlert
Adam Ellis
Molly Finnegan
Eben Freeman
Sarah Gaskins
Bridget Gasper
John Gertsen
Anthony Giglio
Jeff Grdinich
Beth Gruitch
Ted Haigh
Ed Hamilton
Karen Hatfield

John Henry
Robert Hess
Leslie Higgs
Jenny Holcomb
Ryan Huber
Christopher Israel
Aaron Johnson
Ted Kilgore
Jason Kosmas
Francesco Lafranconi
Anne Le
Greg Lindgren
Katie Loeb
Kevin Ludwig
David Lusby
Ryan Magarian
Kevin Mahan
Tobey Maloney
Ryan Maybee
Ryan McGrale
David McLean
Peter Meehan
Junior Merino
Anistatia Miller
Brian Miller
David Nepove

Gerrit Ostermick
Josie Packard
Juliette Pope
Gary Regan
Julie Reiner
Ann Rogers
Kelly Ronan
Audrey Saunders
Joseph Schwartz
Valerie Simi
Todd Smith
LeNell Smothers
Chad Solomon
Ray Srp
Tim Staehling
David Sturno
Bernie Sun
Jamil Tealer
Dominic Venegas
Kieran Walsh
Michael Waterhouse
Thomas Waugh
Neyah White
Rob Willey
Dave Wondrich

Recipe Index

FOOD&WINE
B O O K S

More books from
FOOD & WINE

Best of the Best
The best recipes from the 25 best
cookbooks of the year.

Annual Cookbook 2007
An entire year of recipes.

Wine Guide 2007
The most up-to-date guide with more
than 1,000 recommendations.

FOOD&WINE